T. S Preston

Gethsemani

Meditations on the last day on earth of our blessed redeemer

T. S Preston

Gethsemani
Meditations on the last day on earth of our blessed redeemer

ISBN/EAN: 9783741110931

Manufactured in Europe, USA, Canada, Australia, Japa

Cover: Foto ©Lupo / pixelio.de

Manufactured and distributed by brebook publishing software (www.brebook.com)

T. S Preston

Gethsemani

GETHSEMANI.

MEDITATIONS ON THE LAST DAY ON EARTH

OF

OUR BLESSED REDEEMER.

BY

THE RIGHT REV. MONSIGNOR T. S. PRESTON, V.G., LL.D.,
Prothonotary Apostolic.

SECOND EDITION.

NEW YORK:
ROBERT CODDINGTON,
246 FOURTH AVENUE.

1890.

Dedication.

DEDICATED

TO

MY DEAR CHILDREN IN RELIGION, LOVERS OF JESUS,
AND SPOUSES OF THE HEAVENLY BRIDEGROOM,

AND

To the Sacred Memory

OF THOSE WHO HAVE GONE BEFORE ME
TO THEIR REST IN HIS ARMS.

PREFACE.

THIS little book is a companion to "The Watch on Calvary," which was published two years ago. It begins with the scenes of the last day of Our Lord's life, and follows Him to the garden of Gethsemani, and thence to Calvary. The two books of meditation form a continuous story of the Passion in all its leading particulars. Utterly inadequate as human words are to describe the fearful anguish of our dearest Redeemer, the imperfect attempt here made may, with the blessing of God, assist some souls in the study of the cross, which is the science of saints. It may be my de-

PREFACE.

fect, but I cannot write of Our Lord's sufferings in the ordinary style. I have tried to place the lover of Jesus in sight of the sorrows which he describes, and have given place to the affections which the heart prompts. It was a great consolation to me to know that the "Watch on Calvary" was appreciated by some souls who are seeking to live in constant communion with the Sacred Heart. And it was really at the solicitation of some of my children in religion that I undertook the more difficult task of writing meditations upon the inconceivable agony of Jesus. Therefore to them I dedicate the little work, and I rely upon their prayers that our most compassionate Master may in mercy bless this poor effort to His greater glory and the sanctification of souls.

And I recall the sacred memory of those who have gone before me to their celestial Spouse. Though they are far from me in the presence of the King, yet are they also near me by prayer and mutual love of Him who is indeed our All. They form a part of my life, they will not forget my needs, and they are my intercessors before the throne. We live not in the presence of things seen, but in the realization of things unseen and eternal.

So in utter self-abasement, and simple reliance upon God, I commend this "Gethsemani" to the patient and merciful Heart of Jesus.

T. S. P.

Octave of the Epiphany, 1887.

CONTENTS.

MEDITATION FIRST.
The Garden of Gethsemani, ... 11

MEDITATION SECOND.
The Agony of Fear, ... 67

MEDITATION THIRD.
The Agony of Loneliness, ... 92

MEDITATION FOURTH.
The Agony of Sadness, ... 115

MEDITATION FIFTH.
The Agony of Pain, ... 141

MEDITATION SIXTH.
The Agony of a Wounded Heart, ... 165

MEDITATION SEVENTH.
Jesus Condemned to Death, ... 201

MEDITATION EIGHTH.
The Way to Calvary, ... 275

MEDITATION FIRST.

THE GARDEN OF GETHSEMANI.

MEDITATION FIRST.

THE GARDEN OF GETHSEMANI.

"When Jesus had said these things, He went forth with His disciples over the brook Cedron, where there was a garden, into which He entered."—St. John xviii. 1.

"And He saith to His disciples: Sit you here while I pray. And He taketh Peter, James, and John with Him. And He saith to them: Stay you here and watch."—St. Mark xiv. 32, 33, 34.

THERE was a night in the life of our beloved Redeemer unequalled in its deep darkness by any night this world has ever known. There have been nights of physical darkness when created light seemed to be lost, and the pall of terror has covered the earth. There have been, and there shall be, "signs in the sun and in the moon and in the stars; and upon the earth distress of nations, when men wither away for fear and expectation of what shall come upon the whole world."* There have been, and there shall be, to many souls nights of sorrow so profound that the intelligence seems buried in depths of woe, where created life is a mockery and the light uncreated is hidden, where some unseen hand with fearful agony touches the strings of the aching heart, where nothing less than divine power holds the soul that it may suffer. There are nights when the ties of the creature are snapped asunder, and the earth is turned again to a chaos. There are nights when the spouses of Jesus Christ are in their Gethsemani, and the Beloved cannot be found. They seek Him among the Olive shades, and find Him not. They call out in anguish: "O Thou that dwellest in the gardens! make me hear Thy voice." "Arise, my Love, my Beautiful One, make haste and

* St. Luke xxi. 25, 26.

come." "My dove in the clefts of the rock, show me Thy face, let Thy voice sound in my ears."* There is no response, no sign of His presence; and the storm beats upon the soul as it sinks in the gloom and cries out: "O my Father! if it be possible let this chalice pass from me!" †

Yet what are these nights compared to that which settled upon the Man of Sorrows, the Son of God, when He entered into the garden, bidding the light He created depart, and with the majesty of a God welcoming the waves of superhuman woe and the storms of diabolical rage to beat upon Him! I have watched on Calvary, where He was dying for love of me. The earth trembled as if all things sensible were unanchored, and the powers of heaven were shaken. The cloud covered me, and its gloom sank into the depths of my being. I seemed to die

* Canticles II. 10, 13, 14. † St. Matt. xxv. 39.

and pass with spirits disembodied to a world I knew not. Yet there upon a cross He hung. I could see at times His face through my tears. I could almost see His smile amid His agony. And there amid the darkness so profound, amid the dashing waves of a storm that nearly robbed me of my reason, I heard His voice. He was mighty to save. He seemed to hold in His hand the storm and to be a conqueror all majestic and divine, even when His dying throes shook the cross. Yes, He, my Love, my God, was there in victory. He was dying, but He was there.

Now I see another sight, and I know not how to tell it. It is not Calvary. There is no band of soldiers here. I hear no blaspheming cry. I see no spear nor nail. There is a silence that moves my intellect and heart, and crushes me with its gloom. My Master and my God seems broken. He trembles with fear.

GETHSEMANI.

Oh! it is awful to see Him on whom I lean for every strength tremble so! He is so sorrowful and so sad that if I look at Him my heart breaks, and a sadness all unearthly overwhelms me. Then He looks at me with such a grief in His blessed eyes that I am almost dying. I hear Him say: "My soul is sorrowful even unto death; stay you here and watch with Me." I see Him fall upon the ground. I hear His sighs. I see His tears. I listen to His piteous prayers. My earth is indeed shaken to its centre. The hands of angels hold me up, else I could not live and look upon this sight. Ah! He is bleeding now, bleeding from every pore, all alone, without a foe around Him—bleeding, as it seems, to death. Oh! this is my God, the Lover of my soul, my Beautiful One in His crimson robe! The bleeding hands, that now seem so weak, are my only guides. If I lose my hold of them I shall wander from the path of life. That broken Heart, from which gushes forth the all-atoning blood, is my only refuge. If I cannot rest upon it there is no healing for my wounds; there can come no morning to my night of sorrow or of death.

Dearest Lord, let me draw near, all unworthy as I am! Let me kneel and watch with Thee, where, in tearful sympathy and loving adoration, I may learn something of Thine agony. Here are depths that God alone can sound. It is the anguish of the Infinite. Yet Thou art man like me. And Thou art mine. Thy Blood hath washed me from my sin. Thy Flesh hath quickened my humanity. If I live, it is because Thou livest in me. To know Thee as Thou art is my life; to be like Thee, my only hope of heaven. Open, then, to me the treasures of Thine intelligence. Let its rays descend upon my feeble heart. Thy night is brighter than the day at noon. Thou art the sun of the celestial sphere, and from Thine eclipse Thou canst teach me the lessons which Thy meridian splendor would have preached in vain. Do I dare where even angels fear to come? Am I presumptuous to intrude within the secret of Thy sorrow? When apostles slept and could not see Thine awful chalice, shall one like me be so bold as dare to watch and stay with Thee? Am I able to look upon Thy sweat of blood? Can I venture to look within Thy bursting heart? Can I look upon Thy weeping eyes? Dare I tell the thoughts which crowd upon my mind, and even speak to other souls the lessons of this awful night?

O my most compassionate Lord! it is only for Thy love. It is because Thou art so winning in Thy crimson robe. It is that here Thou dost draw souls to Thee as nowhere else. Here Thou dost espouse them, and the tie is sealed with blood. Oh! forgive me if I err. I would not wound Thee for all that even heaven could give. If Thou wilt teach me and inspire my words, they shall be the adoration of my utter nothingness, the voices of my deep contrition for mine unworthiness. My heart shall ache with Thine that I have been the burden of Thine anguish, that the red drops so freely flowing must touch my wounds and wash my guilt away. Then "Thou shalt sprinkle me with hyssop, and I shall be cleansed; Thou shalt wash me, and I shall be made whiter than snow. To my hearing Thou shalt give joy and gladness, and the bones that have been humbled shall rejoice. Thou shalt deliver me from blood. Thou shalt open my lips, and my mouth shall declare Thy praise. My afflicted spirit shall be a sacrifice to Thee. My contrite and humbled heart Thou wilt not despise."*

* Psalm l. 9-20.

Let me, then, recall the awful scenes of this night. Let me follow my Lord as He enters the Garden of Gethsemani, where He so often kept His watch of prayer. Let me enter with Him, and there, alone with Him, let my heart awake. The saddest of all vigils is at hand. I will remember all. It was the last evening of His life. Three-and-thirty years were nearly spent; those wondrous years of God Incarnate were drawing to their close. They had all led here. Surely, then, this earth was the centre of the universe. It would seem as if the shining stars looked down, and worlds on worlds were marching in their courses, in mute adoration of their King so lowly and so humbled. The Creator held them in His hand as they moved in unmeasured space and glorified His will. Yet He, the King and Crown of all, so bowed down, a man despised and ignored, hides His heavenly splendor where want and sorrow are His daily food. The manger of Bethlehem, the exile in Egypt, the hidden life amid the toils of Nazareth, the wonderful ministry, miracles of charity and grace, all led here. The rising and setting suns that marked the days of God on earth have nearly done their work. Slowly sinks the sun to its evening shades, and darkness is approaching. It must have been unlike the closing of other days. The sun must have trembled as for the last time its departing rays shone upon the face of its Creator about to die. The darkness that came must have been filled with sadness, as if the whole earth were about to be a grave. Yes, it is the last day on earth of Jesus! How did He spend it? What were the words and deeds of this last evening? Precious to the lover are the last moments of the Beloved. How did this Sun of justice and of mercy go down? Let me gather up the last rays of its decline. On this final day there was a wonderful change in the face and form and bearing of my Beloved. The sweetness of heaven dwelt upon Him and spoke from every look and feature. There was a tenderness in all He said and did which was unlike the gentleness of former days. It seemed as if His heart were bursting with love, as if He were to say farewell and could not speak the word. The sadness that clothed Him was too deep for human eyes to read; but it made Him so winning that love mounted to the heights of adoration when it looked upon Him. Surely one day like this should have drawn all hearts, should have conquered every rebel will. He went to the house in Bethany where true hearts had often given rest to His wearied head. Once more the Magdalen shall claim her privilege. Her love and sympathy shall ease His heart; her touch shall soothe His aching head. Once she

poured the ointment upon His blessed
feet, when the tears of her repentance
flowed so fast that He forgave her sin
and washed its guilt away. Now that
she is His, she shall dare to touch His
sacred head. There where the blows of
scorn shall fall, where the crown of thorns
shall make its feverish wounds, the ointment shall be poured. The touch of love
adoring, love above the love of man, shall
speak to the precious face so soon to be
scarred and bruised as if there were none
to care, none to do Him reverence. With
what affection and tenderness does the
penitent kneel before Him! To her quick
perceptions there is something never before seen in His look and in every movement. Even the tones of His voice are
changed. He is the same, and yet there
is a kind of transformation. His heart is
overburdened, and His eyes seem to look
far beyond the things of sense. Some
terrible grief is upon Him which the quick

eyes of love can see in that face always full of the divine serenity, but now looking in all its infinite peace as if He were hurt to the depths of His soul. How can she comfort Him now? There are no words. The crushed heart has no language. In memory of the blessed scene that opened to her the gates of life and gave her again the innocence of youth, she seeks once more the precious ointment. It will tell all. It is the language of her love: "My Master, if I loved Thee then, oh! what art Thou to me now that I have given Thee all my heart, that I have tasted of Thy sweetness, that my whole being is bound up in Thee!" So from her hands flows the ointment upon the sacred head. It fills the precious hair; it runs down upon the majestic forehead; it bedews the blessed face. The Master feels the touch of sympathy, and the incense of her love brings new tenderness to His eyes as they look upon her with a new affection and smile through tears. They seem to say: "O child redeemed by My blood, washed by My hands, and bound to Me now by holiest ties, little dost thou know the way of sorrow that is before Me. You could not go with Me where I would not even take My Mother. I must go alone. I am going to die a cruel death. This is My last day among the children I have come to save. But oh! this farewell, this death were little to the sorrows of this night. They are coming fast. I feel their power now. I am hardly now Myself, they overwhelm Me so. Do you know what your dear hands have done? You have anointed Me for the silent grave. To-morrow night you will seek Me in the sepulchre. My limbs shall lie upon the stone. My hands and feet, all torn and swollen from the nails, shall be cold in death. My heart, whose tremulous beating you can feel, shall be pierced with the soldier's spear. This head you have prepared for its resting-place within the tomb. The face you love shall be bruised with blows. The crown of thorns shall leave its cruel wounds where now your ointment flows. These eyes shall have no more tears to shed; they shall be closed within the grave. Look at Me, My precious child, and wonder not that I am sad. But all of this My death you may see. You may follow in the steps of her I love beyond all save God. You may come and see Me die. But where I go this night you cannot come, and I cannot tell you of its woe. Before I die there is something worse than death. My last night shall be a night indeed. The Eternal Spirit and the angels who are set to guard My humanity are bearing Me now to the garden of My sorrow. Oh! how fast the hours are running! I can hardly now restrain My sweat of blood. I must go. Farewell until you meet Me on Calvary. I must fulfil My heart's desire, make My testament, and leave My legacy of love. Then in My short, suffering life I have done all that even God can do. You have heard the murmurs of My disciple. He has grudged the waste of this anointing. He cannot see the wounds he so unfeelingly inflicts upon Me. He has no knowledge of My grief, no compassion for a heart like Mine, that shrinks and trembles at ingratitude. Even now he has gone to sell Me to My enemies; and he My friend, whom I have kissed, will come to break upon My scene of agony, and with a band of ruffians he will seize Me as I faint beneath the Olive shades. I am God. I am his friend. He will sell Me for a price. I am valued at thirty pieces of silver. He will make his bargain, and he will betray Me with a kiss. Now while I leave you, and with the few who are true to Me pass on to celebrate the mystic rite which this night shall find its first fulfilment, he has done his work. I am sold. Then he will come to the supper of the Passover and sit beside Me. Oh! tell me, was ever sorrow like to Mine?"

With eyes that strained their powers to see the last vision of her Love, the Magdalen followed Him as with His disciples He slowly passed away. Then, when she could see Him no longer, and there was no relief for her aching heart, she fell upon her knees in prayer, and all this awful night she watched, while grief as from another world engulfed her within its shadows. It was her night of agony with Him, although so far away and she so helpless to console Him.

We follow Him as He goes along the way to Jerusalem. In after-years how those disciples remembered the steps of this sad journey! He spoke but little. His form was bent. Now and then He would lean upon St. Peter or St. John, and seem to gather comfort from their truth. His eyes were often filled with tears. And as the Holy City with its temple came in sight, His sobs could not be restrained. The King was coming to His regal city, not amid hosannas or the cries of welcome, but as a stranger to the home which had forsaken Him. The cries of "Crucify Him!" should sound to-morrow, and He was coming there to die. The hill of sacrifice was near. The scene of to-morrow's tragedy was close at hand, and the cross was already hewn and ready. He entered within the city's gates. It was the eve of the great festival, and amid the throngs no one noticed the Nazarene and His poor followers. He passes through the narrow street. The house is open and the room is prepared. "His time is near at hand." No power can stay the fleeting hours. The sun has set, and the darkness of the evening is upon them, when they enter there to celebrate the Passover. Once when the destroying angel stood to bring the curse of death upon their homes, the blood of a bleeding lamb was their preserver. Now the Lamb is here, Himself to keep the feast, and then fulfil the type and complete the prophecy. Around that table they are seated, the apostles of the New Law, and the Master with them. The Paschal Lamb is set before them. The seven days of unleavened bread were kept. Their shoes were on their feet, their staves were in their hands.* Was this a feast of joy, this memorial of a nation's deliverance? Why, then, the sadness that from the Master fell upon the disciples? Is the dread angel of death hovering over them, and will not the blood of the lamb protect them? Alas! there is a mightier death at hand than earth has ever known. It will strike the Master. The destroyer will meet the

* Exodus xii.

Creator. The Lamb of God, the Eternal Son, is to be slain. The great types of patriarchal days and of the Old Law are now to be fulfilled. While they were eating the Paschal Lamb the face of Jesus fills them with terror and apprehension of evil to come. A death-like paleness rests upon it, and life seems to be departing from Him. He seems to take the place of the lamb before them. They are feeding upon it now. Soon they shall feed upon Him. Yet there is a pause for a moment, as the mystic rite is finished, and He turns with eyes full of unearthly agony, to look upon the disciples. "Are you not My friends in My dire extremity? Will you stand between Me and the shadows of horror which pursue Me? I must tell you of the sorrow which breaks my heart as now I make My dying testament. One of you, My chosen whom I have so loved, is about to betray Me. He has partaken of the

Paschal Lamb with Me, and, traitor that he is, he will even partake of *Me* and feed upon the body and the blood in My last testament of love, the sacred humanity of his Master and his God, which he with the price of treason has delivered unto death. Do you wonder that I am sad? You have been with Me in the toils and sorrows of My ministry. You have seen My miracles and heard the words which I have spoken to no other ears. We have been a little band bound by the ties of a more than human friendship. The world has hated Me, and priests have sought My life. You have known Me as I have revealed to you My Godhead. You have been My comfort when the multitude has mocked Me and the rulers have driven Me to the mountain or the desert. Now the chosen band is broken: Fresh from My embrace the traitor goes, and he will find Me in

My wonted place of prayer, and the shadows of the olive-trees shall see to-night the breaking heart of God's incarnate Son. The traitor is at My side; he dips his hand in the dish with Me. He even looks upon My agonizing face with untroubled eyes, while your true hearts are full of sympathy and strange dismay. He asks Me to tell him of the treason which he feigns to wonder at. I give him now his last warning. I shall not speak again to him until I meet him in the garden, and My blood-stained lips receive his sacrilegious kiss. Will he dare remain, now that he hears the voice of My reproach? Will he, too, kneel while I shall change the bread and wine by My creating power? Will he, too, feed upon the Lamb of Calvary, upon My Body and My Blood?"

Now may the Spirit tell the scene. I see the disciples as they kneel with hearts o'erwhelmed and heads bowed down. But I cannot paint my Master as He stands before that table. The scene is more than earthly. He takes upon Himself the majesty of God, and yet He wears the utmost humility of man. I see before me the grandeur of the patriarchal line, the dignity of my first father Adam, the form sublime of Noe as he stood upon the mountain when the destroying waves sank away and the baptized earth slowly emerged from the waste of waters. I see the great high-priest Aaron in his sacerdotal robes, with the long line of Levites as they stood within the tabernacle and the temple before the altar of propitiation. I see Melchisedech, king of Salem, prince of peace, "without father, without mother, without genealogy, having neither beginning of days nor end of life, but likened unto the Son of God, a priest for ever."* I see more than this. The

* Heb. vii. 3.

past by mystery becomes the present. I see the chaos of the new-created earth. The light of the Eternal Spirit hangs upon it, and the Word of the Father speaks, while celestial light springs forth and the mountains and the valleys put on their forms of beauty. It is my lowly Master. I know well the blessed face. And yet it seems another. Before the sight my heart, my soul, my whole being bow down and sink in wonder as I listen. It is the same voice, and yet its tones are unlike the tones of human voice. I fall prostrate before the tender revelation of my Master's heart and the words that come from the throne of Father, Son, and Holy Ghost, from between the wings of Cherubim, from the uncreated light. This is His dying testament. This is His legacy of love. This is "the priest for ever according to the order of Melchisedech."* He takes the bread; He lifts

* Heb. vii. 17.

his eyes to heaven; He blesses it; He gives it to His disciples. The lips of the Creator speak: "Take ye and eat; this is My Body." "He takes the chalice; He blesses it; He lifts His voice in praise. He gives it to the kneeling twelve: Drink ye all of this, for this is My Blood of the new testament, which shall be shed for many for the remission of sins." * When this mighty miracle was wrought I looked upon the sad faces of the twelve. There was Peter with his strong faith and the light of a new zeal kindling in his earnest eyes. There was John with more than human tenderness gazing upon the face divine, seeking to read its wealth of love as in its changing features there flashed the light of Godlike power with the softness of pity infinite. I watched the wondering disciples, then lifted to the exalted dignity of their priesthood. In each

* St. Matt. xxvi. 26-28.

I saw a transformation strange as it was wonderful. There was a tie before unknown, before impossible. The Master and the chosen band were one indeed, partakers of the One. The New Testament was proclaimed. The priests had feasted on the Lamb of God. "There was one Body and one Bread." * And yet a veil of darkness fills the sacred place. They cannot see the fulness of the mighty gift of God. "What I do thou knowest not now; but thou shalt know hereafter," † were the words of Jesus, which were well remembered in the days to come. I looked upon the face of Judas. Does he hate his Master now? Is it madness like that of demons, or is it the blackness of despair? It is no merely human face. He has added to his treason the crime which has no equal in the vileness of untruth. He has received the Lamb whom he

* 1 Cor. x. 17.   † St. John xlii. 7.

has sold for gain. The very body which he has sought to hang upon the cross he has not feared to take within his lips. Will he not yet repent? Is it yet too late for pardon? I see no signs of sorrow. His eyes are bold. His hands are firm. His limbs tremble not with fear. Will he go upon his errand now? The shadows deepen. The midnight hour approaches. The priests are waiting on his word before the festal rites begin.

No! there is another scene. It shall prepare him for his work. My eyes were full of tears. My heart was overwhelmed. There was a sadness deep as darkest night, and yet a sweetness like a breath of peace from Paradise. I loved this sadness, even though my heart seemed breaking. Through my tears I looked upon my Master. What is it that draws me so and yet which makes me tremble? He is more winning than I have ever known Him, and yet the change alarms me so. I must look upon Him, and yet I quake with fear. There is a look as of one slain, as of one sacrificed and yet alive. I cannot speak. I cannot move. I can only look upon Him. Where will He lead me? My soul, without words, cries out: "Draw me, O my Beloved; we will run after Thee to the odor of Thine ointments." * "He rises from the table and layeth aside His garments, and, taking a towel, He girds Himself therewith. He poureth water into a basin, and begins to wash the feet of the disciples, and to wipe them with the towel wherewith He was girded."† I hear Him say: "If I wash thee not, thou hast no part in Me." I see the special love wherewith He touches every one of the disciples. These are the feet that for Him shall stand upon the dark mountains of the earth, and to its utmost

* Canticles I. 3.   † St. John xiii. 2, 3.

bounds proclaim His grace. These are the feet that in their turn shall run with joy to the sacrifice of blood. He comes to Judas now. Will he, too, let the Master wash his feet? Can he bear the tender touch? And will the feet which these hands have cleansed run now to seal the fatal bargain? Where are the wings of angels? Where the powers of grace? My Jesus looks upon him once again as He rises from his feet. It is a look that might have moved the adamant. It tells him of the fearful sorrows of ingratitude, of the guilt of treason, of the chance of pardon. That hard face has no relenting feature. It changes not beneath the tearful gaze of a sorrowing God. O Judas! awake before thy doom is sealed. Canst thou betray thy friend and benefactor, and for a paltry price canst thou sell thy Master? There is no relenting. A film of gloom comes down upon his eyes. He can hardly see. The light of reason falls a slave to avarice, and tenderest ties are broken at the voice of passion. O false disciple! it is too late. The lips of Jesus open once again. I never heard His voice so sad. Not even on the cross were His tones so filled with grief. "If thou, My child, whom I have loved with love that God alone can give, whom I have made My priest, to whom the treasures of My heart have been unveiled—if, after all that has passed in the secret of our friendship, thou wilt deliver Me to Mine enemies who seek My blood, then hasten on thy way. They that have bought Me and will kill Me are waiting for thee. It is an awful deed, but spare Me not. Let the knife of thine ingratitude go deep within My heart. If thou dost not shrink to thrust it there, go on thy fearful way. 'What thou doest, do quickly.' " * I saw the traitor go, and with him went the heavy cloud

---

* St. John xiii. 27.

which filled the souls of all. The shades of sadness for a moment passed from the Master's face, as when the light of heaven for an instant drives away the darkness of a gathering storm. The heart of Jesus seems relieved. There is no treason now around Him: only friends are kneeling at His feet. He hath many parting words to speak. He tells them of His sacrifice and its fruits, of the Church which they shall found, of the love wherewith the Father shall embrace them for His sake. They have seen the body of their God made flesh. They shall see the body mystical which His humanity shall quicken into life eternal. He tells them of that sacrament of unity wherein all made one with Him shall be one with God; of the Spirit that shall come upon them to unfold the riches which they could not comprehend. His eyes are filled with radiance divine as He beholds the Church which, coming from His opened side, shall be the mother of the living.

He lifts His eyes to heaven, and His lips ejaculate a prayer: "Father, the hour is come; glorify Thy Son, that Thy Son may glorify Thee."* He seems ready now for the sacrifice. I listen as a hymn of praise arises from the Master and the wondering disciples. His voice, so dear and so divine, is leading in the melody, and the sadness that broke forth in tears now breaks forth in song. Oh! when shall a hymn like this be heard again? "When Israel went out of Egypt, and the house of Jacob from a barbarous people, Judea was made his sanctuary, Israel his dominion. The sea saw and fled; Jordan was turned back. At the presence of the Lord the earth was moved, at the presence of the God of Jacob." "The sorrows of death have compassed me, and the perils of hell have found

* St. John xvii. 1.

me." "I will take the chalice of salvation and call upon the name of the Lord." "The stone which the builders rejected, the same is become the head of the corner. This is the gate of the Lord: the just shall enter therein."* Is this like the melody of heaven? When shall I hear my Jesus sing once more?

But I must follow the steps of my Beloved. The scene within the cenacle is over. With the solemn chant He passes out upon the open street. In the darkness of the night they walk unmolested towards the gate of the city, and their voices are clear upon the still air. Above them all I can hear my Master's tones as He leads them towards the Mountain of Olives. Those blessed tones are now sad, now trembling with fear, now even joyful. Oh! tell me, my angel guardian, where is my Beloved going? My Mother is not here. I look in vain for her gentle face

---

* Psalms cxiii., cxiv., cxv., cxvii.

and the strength that ever held my faltering steps. Can I go where she is not? Yes, I must follow my Jesus. He draws me and I must go. I trust Him for His grace. "Even if I walk in the midst of the shadow of death, I can fear no evil while He is with me." * I may be bold, I may be presuming, but I must go. They are coming now to the brook Cedron, and they lead me into the garden of Gethsemani. Well do I know its recesses and its Olive shades. Here I have often been with my Master, and I have watched Him in His prayer. At a distance I have seen Him hide Himself beneath the trees, and I have begged for the inspiration of His soul and that I might unite my feeble voice with His. But this is not like other nights. This is the last; and to-morrow my Love will die. I fear and tremble, and my heart is beating as if its life would quickly run out; but can I

* Psalm xxii. 4.

stay away? I will follow Him. I will not intrude upon His gaze. There are angels here in serried ranks. There are the spirits of the night. I feel their power, and I am borne along, I know not how. My angel shall help me. He shall hide me beneath his wings while my Jesus makes his watch of prayer on this His last night on earth. He will forgive me, for it is love that leads me, and love that cannot be rebuked. With trembling steps my Master leads the way into the dense shade, where the light of the Paschal moon can scarcely penetrate. Then He pauses, and it seems that He can no longer stand. His whole form bends forward as if he were about to fall. He sighs. He weeps. He looks to His disciples with an expression of the most terrible suffering, as if begging them to pity Him. He leans upon Peter, and then bows His head upon the breast of the beloved disciple. Oh! is He dying now?

He turns to the eleven to speak. His
sobs choke His utterance. "Pray, pray,"
said He, "for the tempter cometh, and
his angels are here in power. The dreadful gloom of their lost spirits is upon Me.
Stay you here, but pray for strength,
while I go yonder to my awful prayer. I
saw it from all eternity. I saw it when
first I opened My eyes upon this sinful
world, when first I laid My head upon
the dear breast of My mother. I dread it,
but it must come. Stay you here, and as
you can, unite your prayers with Mine.
And you, Peter, the rock of My Church,
My vicar upon earth; and you, John My
beloved, and James, who have asked to
sit upon My throne, and have thought
yourselves able to be baptized with blood
—you come with Me; come, and leave Me
not alone; come and watch with Me. Oh!
I am so sad. Do you know what it is for
Me, your God, to be so sad? The great
capacities of My divine soul are strained

to their utmost. My soul, the soul of the Incarnate Word, is sorrowful even unto death."

O my Jesus! what will I do? I cannot live and see Thee suffer so. Oh! what is it? There is no foe at hand. Earth is quiet. I hear nothing but the plaintive murmur of the trees. Surely no enemy can come nigh Thee in this secure retreat. But where are the angels that ever watch around Thee? Are they frightened when they see Thy sorrowing face? Come and help me, spirits of the light; come, lift my eyes and hold me up. I thought I could always look upon my Redeemer's face. If He would permit me I thought my eyes would ever yearn to meet His gaze. Now He does not hinder me. He even courts my look of sympathy. He even asks me to turn to Him with all my powers of sense and sight. And yet I cannot look upon Him. Such sorrow, such sadness, such awful loneliness are written on the features I love so well, that I am not able to lift up my head; and when for an instant my tearful eyes meet His, my head bows down in utter weakness. I know He sees my heart. I cannot, oh! I cannot look upon this agony of my God. It is worse than death. I can hardly feel that I am living, and yet I am not dead. He trembles so that my reason seems to stagger. My God! the strength of all my hopes is overwhelmed with fear. I see Peter, James, and John, and they are resting on the ground. Oh! can they sleep? And He, so lonely, so pitiful, staggers on as if there were no friend to comfort Him. O my God! hold Him up; send forth Thine angels to bear Him in their hands, or He will fall! Alas! it is too late! What shall I do? A nameless terror freezes me, and my hands and feet will not obey my will. He has fallen on His face. My Beautiful One, my beloved Lord, has fallen as if

He were bereft of life. There He lies as helpless as if He were dead. Oh! tell me, is He dead? I looked forward to the hill of sacrifice. I was to go to Calvary to see Him die. Is it all over now? Here in the garden, without the touch of nail or spear, is He dead? Ah! I hear the blessed tones of that loved voice. My spirit wakes from its dread dream. He is not dead. But oh! what do I hear? In tones so weak, so full of grief, I hear Him say, "O My Father! if it is possible let this chalice pass from Me. Nevertheless, not as I will but as Thou wilt." These are the words which come from His dear mouth, pressed upon the ground as if He could not raise His head. Oh! in all my experience or imagination of human woe I had never dreamed of sorrow like this. All the agonies which the frenzy of men or demons has caused the martyrs in their death-struggles are nothing to this! Even He, the mighty God, the strong arm of the Most High, can hardly bear it. Even *He* begs that this chalice of sorrow may pass from Him. That plaintive cry, that wail of the broken heart of my Lord, pierces my soul. I seem to lose all power over my reason. I tremble so that I seem like one dying. O my Jesus, my All, my only Rest! what can I do for Thee? Thou holdest me up with the embrace of Thy loving arms, and Thou art prostrate upon the ground as if there were none to comfort Thee! Oh! so desolate is my Beloved that He is alone in this His hour of superhuman woe. Do my tears reach Thee? Do the sighs of my grateful heart come near Thee now? Alas! God have mercy on me, I fear I have my part in this agony of my only Love—I can weep; I can pray; but I am not worthy to come near my Beautiful One in His awful disfigurement. I have to beg the breaking Heart of my Jesus to pity me.

Where is Magdalen with the sweet ointment of her true love? Where is my blessed Mother, whose look or touch would have soothed His sorrow? Oh! she could not be here. He loved her too much to take her into this Gethsemani. Could she bear it? She has to nerve herself for the morrow, for Calvary, for the death-scene, for the burial. What is my little love to hers? It is only as a drop to the vast ocean, or as one ray of light to the meridian splendor of the sun. Where is the beloved disciple, he whose head had so often rested on the sacred breast, where now the heart is struggling with its tumultuous beating? Could he go away from his Lord? I heard the Master say, as He left him amid the shadows: "Stay here and watch with Me." Oh! is he watching now? I see no one. My Beloved lies alone upon the green turf, with no one to watch His convulsive sobs, the awful trembling of

His prostrate body. The grass of Gethsemani takes up His tears, and the silent trees are the only visible companions of His agony. Not a leaf moves; not a breath stirs the foliage which droops around Him, as if even nature were dead. O death! O cruel death! where hast thou had a triumph like this?

As I watch, behold He rises slowly, so weak that He can only stagger along. He goes pitifully to His chosen friends. He seems, like a beggar, to yearn for their sympathy, and His tearful eyes, so red with weeping, seem to crave a look of kindness or a word of love. Alas! their eyes are closed in sleep. Upon the ground they lie, all unconscious of His terrible grief. They could sleep while He was suffering in mortal agony. O my poor Jesus! I see Thee in the letters of prophecy "looking sadly about when there is none to help, seeking with sobs for aid and finding none,"* not even one kind look or word. "He appears as the most abject of men, and as one despised, like a leper, struck by God and afflicted."† "He called for friends, and they deceived Him"; "His eyes have failed with weeping," and His broken form and agonizing face speak without words: "O all ye that pass by the way, attend and see if there be any sorrow like unto Mine. The Lord has made a vintage of Me, as He spoke in the day of His fierce anger." He hath been trodden in the wine-press alone, and the red drops are forcing themselves from His crushed heart to every pore of His body. "From above the fire hath burned in His bones. The anger of God hath chastised Him, and made Him desolate, wasted with sorrow."‡ He looks at His sleeping friends. It would seem that such a look from God incarnate in His

* Isaias lxiii. 5.   † Ibid. 3, 4.   ‡ Lam. i. 12, 13.

woe would have roused them from sleep and have stirred the depths of their being. No! they are resting as if unmoved. There comes a change in His countenance, and in the look of utter desolation there is an expression of pity with ineffable tenderness. He speaks to Peter, who a few moments ago was ready to die with Him. Oh! if I could remember for all eternity that look of His face and the tones of His voice! It went to my heart and opened the fountains of remorse. It wounded me with the sting of its sad reproach. I know that wound will never heal. I ask not for its healing until I see Him in glory, and the pierced hands shall touch it when there can be no longer danger of parting from my Love. "Peter, My true disciple, My vicar on earth, is it so that thou canst sleep now? I begged you with tears to watch with Me. Could you not watch one hour?" "Alas! you know not your danger. You have not begun to learn the tenderness of My heart. This is an awful night. The powers of darkness are crowding around us. The sins of the ages are weighing Me down. Arise, awake, watch and pray. Pray as you never prayed before. The spirit may be willing, but poor human nature, how weak it is!"

He turns away, and, as if borne by some supernatural force, staggers back to the lonely scene of desolation. The darkness deepens. A superhuman gloom falls upon the garden. There are no shadows. It is all black night. I strain my eyes. I can see nothing; but, O my God! I hear Him fall. He falls more heavily than before. Has awful death come at last? No, I feel that the destroying angel is there with his drawn sword. But he has not killed Him yet. In the dense, fearful darkness I hear again His agonizing prayer, more plaintive than before. It must rend the heavens. It must break the clouds. There must come some ray of light. "O My Father! if this chalice cannot pass away except I drink it, Thy will be done." Now I can see nothing, but I seem to see blackness of night. I know not how long my Beloved lay prostrate on the ground. It seemed an age when I looked and saw a shadow pass before me, and I knew it was He. Nothing else could so move me. I follow the shadow. It leads me to the three disciples. They are asleep again. Their eyes are so heavy they can scarcely open them. Some spirit of darkness hath touched them. They are struggling to awake. I saw the bending shadow of my Love. Not a word was spoken. Dreadful sighs rang out upon the chill air and upon my frozen senses. Convulsive sobs shook Him, and the tears ran down like fountains. But I could not see His face. Perhaps He spared me for His great compassion; I think I could not then have seen His face and lived. Yet how I loved Him then I could not tell, fastened though I was and rooted to the ground like the rocks of ages. There were things ineffable of which I cannot speak. I suffered; I seemed to suffer with Him; and yet the love I had for Him was like a fire in which my whole being seemed to burn. May He forgive me! I am dumb before Him. I know not what I say.

The shadow passes by me once again. This time it comes nearer. Was I presumptuous when I thought I felt the power of His presence, and in my grief a sweetness stole upon me such as I had not known before? I dare not say. But He passed, and soon the light, the inward light, had gone. There was no outward light. To the sacred place where my Beloved went I force my vision. O earth, earth, cruel earth, that hearest now the plaintive prayer of God made man! Again hath He fallen on thy breast. The earth which so many sins have cursed shall bear Him when no other place of rest is found, and shall dry His tears and drink His blood. "O my Father! I know Thy will. This chalice which torments Me so, cannot pass away. Not My will but Thine be done. I take it. Press it to My lips, and I will drink it all. My Father, from Thy hand I take in its full measure this awful grief. No one but God could drink it, and I am God, Thy co-equal Son. Let the sword descend, but let the Eternal Spirit hold Me up." Now I hear no more. He will not speak again. I seem to feel the desolation of this awful chalice. He, my Beloved, my Beautiful One—He is drinking it all alone. I know He is not dead, for I feel so strangely the power of His life. Slowly do the moments fly. It seems the watch of an eternal night. There is no sun. There are no stars. There are only clouds which wrap all nature in their gloom.

Yes, my Jesus, I am watching here with Thee. While Thou art here I will not fear the night. I will pray, and when I cannot pray I will think of Thee. And when the power of thought seems gone, and I am as if I had no being, I will *feel* Thy presence. I could not touch Thy chalice. Oh! I am not fit to think that I could be sharer in Thy woe—I, who so many times by my inconstant love have grieved Thee! Yet here, on the darkest night that earth hath ever seen, I would believe that I am weaned from all but Thee, that I will never wound Thee more. And so I pray, while shadows after shadows pass upon my soul, and sense seems lost for ever. At last there comes to me a ray of light. From some far-off source it lightens up the darkness and reveals to me the prostrate form of my agonizing Lord. One beam shines full upon Him. All else is dark. Yet, O my Blessed Lord! what does this light unfold? Thou art bleeding. Thy garments are wet with blood. Thy hands and feet are bleeding. Thy dear face is red, and great drops of blood are running down from Thy weeping eyes. The grass beneath Thee is crimson with the fast-gushing current of Thy life. Oh! what can I do? I close my eyes with fear, with horror, and with grief. Then I dare to look again. I am not deceived. It is too true. The chalice has been taken, and it has done its work. The heart of love divine, of tenderness infinite, gave way. Can I live and see this sight? Angels cannot help me now. Their drooping wings hang down, and they are desolate. Only the bleeding hands can support me here. Prostrate there He lies, and yet I feel the pressure of those almighty arms. "Who is this that cometh from Edom, with dyed garments from Bosra, this Beautiful One in His robe? Why is Thine apparel red, and Thy garments like theirs that tread in the wine-press?"* "This is the Word of God, and He wears the garments sprinkled with blood." † The Infinite is stooping here. The love of God has found its true expression. God is Man and bleeds from head to foot with agony. O Jesus, my redeemer! how I love Thee in Thy sad disfigurement! Let my feeble heart but tell Thee in this night of woe how dear Thou art to me! I love Thee for Thy beauty, which far transcends the powers of thought. I love Thee for Thy grace, which, amid the wrecks my sins have

* Isaias lxiii. 1, 2. † Apoc. xix. 13.

wrought, hath strength to quicken me with life. I love Thee for the pity which Thou hast for me, so lonely and so vile. But most of all I love Thee because Thou wilt have my heart, and in Thy dear compassion dost stoop to take my love. To Thee in Thy great humiliation, exhausted with Thy sweat of blood, I consecrate my all. The ears divine are red with blood, but they are quick to hear my vows. My bleeding Jesus, let me come to Thee. Let my tears run down with Thine. Oh! keep me, wash me in Thy blood!

Now the beam of light which revealed to me my Blessed Love seems to gather strength. It is brighter in my soul. I watch my Jesus, and, oh! eternal praise to God, He is not alone. Bright forms are at His side. Rays of uncreated gladness gleam upon their garments as they draw near. They kneel around Him. They lift Him up. They bow before Him. I hear no words. Yet darkness flies away, and upon His agonizing face there comes a smile of peace. The light of heaven is here, and I must look away. Not for *me* this revelation of the glory that shall be hereafter. These are the great archangels come to speak the words of comfort in the desolation of their Eternal King.

MEDITATION SECOND.

THE AGONY OF FEAR.

MEDITATION SECOND.

THE AGONY OF FEAR.

"Fear seized upon me, and trembling, and all my bones were affrighted."—JOB iv. 14.

I LOOK not now upon the angels who have come so gladly to console my dearest Lord. My heart seems far away. I see one sight—the prostrate form of my Beloved. I see the awful sweat of blood. I see the crimsoned turf whereon He lies. I hear one voice—His sad, His piercing cry. He, so strong, seems now so weak. I feel the watches of His agony, as step by step the fearful waves dash over Him. I see Him overwhelmed with fear, trembling as if some mighty dread would kill Him. His sadness like a pall of darkness falls upon my spirit till I pant for life. I see Him there alone. He is the mighty God; yet never was a sufferer so desolate. No night like this has ever clouded all the rays of light or been so awful in its gloom. And yet I love Thee so, my Jesus, that I cannot turn away. I would fear, if Thou didst leave me here, for surely I am not among the powers of earth. I am not among the dead, nor do I seem to be among the living. This garden is a world unknown. It cannot be the earth. It is not heaven. In the depths of darkness drear my soul is lost in Thee. Thine agonizing heart is drawing me. Wilt Thou, dearest Lord, but listen to my prayer? May one like me but look within the clouds that wrap Thee round? Oh! tell me something of Thy woe. Then Thy garden shades shall be my teacher. Here I see no created thing. None but Thee, my dearest Lord, none but Thee.

GETHSEMANI.

From the prostrate form amid the sighs and tears, while red drops gush from every pore, there comes a message to my heart. My soul awakens; my whole being trembles. Deeper grows the night. I am descending down, down some awful cavern where my loneliness grows sweet, where my desolation with its fearful pain seems death; for here the voice comes up to me which tells me of my Master's woe, and in Gethsemani I am drinking in the sorrows of the Sacred Heart.

Listen, if thou canst, my child. Thou shalt see what thy birth of blood has cost Me. If thou art Mine, I have won thee by a broken heart. Dost thou love Me well enough to follow where I lead? Art thou not afraid to dwell within these shades, the darkness of a superhuman night, and here to be alone with Me, to be alone indeed, where no sense shall tell that I am with thee, where even I shall hide Myself, and faith alone shall prove to thee that I have not forsaken thee? Canst thou lie down upon the crimsoned turf and weep with Me, even when I seem to leave thee all alone? Then, while earth and sense seem dead, and heaven is far away, My sighs shall teach thee. Thou shalt know a little of the depths of My compassion. Thou shalt feel a little of the tenderness which dwells within My breast. Would the nuptials of thy King affright thee if I seal thee to My Heart in blood? I will tell thee of My sufferings when thou art wholly Mine. When I put the ring upon thy hand, and press thee closely to My wounded side, thou shalt learn a little of My love, a little of the grief that overwhelmed My soul, that I might wash thee clean, might win thy heart and make thee all My own.

When I took upon Myself the work of suffering, I took it as a God. I bade the light depart. I bade the torturers to come. I bowed My head and bade the mighty waves of sorrow dash upon Me. The spirits of the rebel host whom once I chased from heaven and bound in everlasting chains were then unloosed. They came for their revenge. Within the hearts of men I came to save they lighted up the fires of hate, and earth arose against Me with demoniac rage. I willed this passion. I willed it as a God. And when the clouds arose I felt the fury of the storm. I trembled with the frenzy of the blast. To devils and to men I was the mark of every weapon, while I held back the drooping wings of angels, and God's incarnate Son sustained the shock alone. Well do I remember that last awful day, My last among the sons of men. I was descending to the pains of death before the soldiers came, before the nails were driven, before My Judas sold Me. There was no disease upon Me. The flesh of God could never know decay. There was perfect health within Me, and the fulness of my manhood crowned Me with its strength. And yet death was coming, awful death, such as this sad world had never known before. It was coming over Me with all its baneful power. My limbs were failing. I could hardly move. My head was aching with the pangs of more than mortal pain. It drooped upon My breast, and tears came freely to My eyes and almost closed My vision. My heart sank down, and agony I cannot tell you of so filled Me that I struggled with this mighty death to wait for Me upon the cross. I held back the bitter waters, and all day long I bade them watch for Me within the garden. There I gave them liberty to overwhelm Me. Yet could I tell you of the love that all that day so filled My trusting heart— love infinite that ran within My veins and gushed unbidden from My eyes? I had loved the race of man eternally, and the tenderness of God was My compassion for the lost. But that last day it seemed something more to Me. When the Magdalen touched My aching head My love was stronger than the pangs of death. I so yearned to clasp My wandering sheep, and hold them safe within My arms, that I welcomed more of woe, and the blood was bounding in My veins, impatient to be shed. And when I journeyed to Jerusalem to die the thought was sweet to Me. Each step was bringing on the hour of grace when by fearful death I could redeem My loved ones, break their chains, and wash them from the stains of guilt. In the Paschal Rite I saw Myself, the grand fulfilment of the type, the Lamb of God upon the cross of Calvary. Indeed, My heart was bleeding then. My one relief, the moment of My perfect joy, was that in which I gave Myself to be the food of My redeemed. The bread I gave them was My Flesh; the chalice was My Blood. I was within them then: My love had found its full expression. Could God do more? I humbly bent Me down and washed the feet of My disciples. My touch was tenderness divine. There was never love like Mine.

Yet time was hastening on. My hour was fast approaching. The sun had set. The stars were hidden. The bitter waters were in waiting for Me. They were to meet Me in Gethsemani. And as I turned to face them deadly fear came over Me. In My chosen place of prayer, in the garden shades, where many nights I watched and with My Father held communion, there I promised them their full dominion. There had I unchained the powers of evil, the spirits of the night. There I covenauted to meet them all alone. Yet, when I led My little band, and even from the rest withdrew My chief apostles as a guard around Me, or at least to watch with Me and grant My breaking heart the consolation of their sympathy, I began to fear and tremble. This dread was not unknown, and yet for Me it was an agony. This was the onset of the bitter waters They dashed upon Me, and I was their sport, as darkness deepened and I cried for loneliness; and the gloom engulfed Me in its rayless night.

Child of My passion, thou hast chosen Me to be thy Spouse: dost thou wonder that I feared? Let Me tell thee as I can of this agony of fear. It is little that My words can speak. There are no words to paint the horror of that hour.

I had bidden all created light depart —the light that cheers the day, the light that softens all the dread of night. It was total darkness on My soul, a heavy weight that pressed me down. And in this gloom were forms of every ill; and every sorrow that has fallen on the heart of man took shape and pressed upon Me. Phantoms drear with demon faces, with the laugh and jeer of hopeless misery, seemed to touch Me and oppress Me with their baneful breath. I heard the wail of every woe that man has known since Paradise was closed, and sorrow lifted up its head to torture and to reign. I felt the reptiles of the earth as with their slimy fangs they seemed to crawl upon Me, to dart their fiery tongues, and sting Me with their poisoned fangs. No grace of things created, no form of beauty, filled the chasm dire wherein I fell; but horrid faces gazed upon Me with the look of hate and scorn. I saw the vast procession of the lost. The charnel-house wherein their bodies lay corrupted seemed My resting-place. Their mouldering bones arose to taunt Me with the noises of the grave and fill my senses with the odor of the tomb. Spirits disembodied, full of fire, smoking with the air of hell, crowded round Me with the curses of despair. The souls I could not save were eager to affright Me with their horrid breath, or touch Me with the lurid flame that burned within them. Then came the rebel host of angels fallen from their high estate. I let them loose. "This was their hour; the power of darkness." "Their name is legion." They rushed upon Me with their sable wings; the fearful gloom of spirits lost was like a mantle of corruption covering Me. They filled the night. I touched them with convulsive trembling. When I put out My hands I felt them there. When I looked within the depths before Me, I saw them stooping over Me as birds unclean descend upon their prey. I heard their curses ringing on the air. Their thirst of ages for revenge was now to satiate itself. And I was before them crushed, and My humanity was broken by their violence, although I am the Son of God. Dost thou wonder that I feared, that My bones were trembling with the horror of the scene, that My quaking heart was nigh to death? Something of this fear My loved have known in paths wherein My grace has led them. But I have never left them in the gloom alone. A night like Mine they could not bear and live. When they have touched the bitter waters I was with them. When they descended to the vale of death My angels went before them, and My hand upheld them in the darkness. Yet I, thy Master and thy God, was all alone.

Then when the waves of sorrow seemed to close upon Me, and the spirits of the night were reigning in the deep that covered Me, I looked upon My body, thus the sport of every power of ill, and saw the way to Calvary, the tortures of the cross. So weak was I that I could hardly raise My head or move a limb. The fever of My blood was burning Me, as the red drops were pouring out from face and hands and feet. I saw the marks of the scourge upon My back; the crown of thorns was pressing in My brain. The cruel nails seemed now to hold Me fast. The cross was on My bleeding shoulders, and I was fainting with the load. I could not walk, and yet My weary way was all before Me. I said in My dismay: O sinner! what art thou doing? This is the body of thy God. These are the hands and feet of God. This aching, thorn-crowned head is God's. Can you, do you dare to mutilate it so? I saw the hill of Calvary. The place of skulls with noisome odor choked My breath. I hung upon My wounds, slowly bleeding to My death, and beside Me were the murderers to fill my dying hours with shame. All the pains of crucifixion seemed to come before the time, and nail and spear transfixed Me as I lay so helpless on the ground. These fearful pangs were not too much to satisfy My yearning love. Within My breast My heart with its pulsations swift was calling for My baptism. And yet when all the morrow came before Me, and every torture one by one I felt, there surged upon Me like a flood of fire the horror of an awful fear. God's only Son, the image of the Father, the brightness of His glory, to be treated so! God made man to be thus despised; to be mocked and scourged ; as a common criminal to be crucified!

Then I looked within the soul divine

ever gazing on the Father's face, the heart whose tenderness is but the pity of the Deity, and upon Me came My agonies in one. I took the cup of man's ingratitude and drank it to the dregs. My heart was open by its love, and here My enemies had found their mark; and where I suffered most, with wanton cruelty they plied the arrows of their hate. I was prostrate on the ground, and yet I seemed to hang upon the cross. I heard the mockery which, with studied insult, followed every shadow of My face and every throb of My convulsions. I prayed for their forgiveness, and the jeer was My response. I already tasted vinegar and gall they pressed upon My parched and feverish lips. I forgave one murderer who hung beside Me. I was the king of murderers then. I lost the other soul. The shadow of My cross, the privilege to die with Me, were not enough to save him from the flames of hell. I saw My priceless Mother, dearer far to Me than all but God. She stood beneath My cross in majesty of woe. It seemed to Me that I had never loved her as I did then. Bethlehem, the desert drear, and Nazareth, the blessed time when I could lay My head upon her loving heart, came back, and the filial tide of love from God's only Son upon her flowed. Mother, Mother! thou canst not know the fulness of My love for thee. There is no such love, and God alone can sound it. I am thy child, it is My dearest earthly joy. I wear thy features, and for all eternity I shall look like thee. But I am thy God, and He alone can know how God can love His Mother. So, when in agony I saw her tears, and knew her heart was breaking too, strange was My crushing fear that she, the dearest of created things, should suffer with Me; that I could never comfort her, nor stay the death that seemed to lay its pall upon her, too, and wrap her in its cold embrace. My dearest must come near My cross of pain; I suffer with them, but I cannot save them from the chalice which I drink.

I saw the sorrow of the Magdalen. Her sobs like arrows pierced My soul. I had washed her from all stain, but little did she know the cost to Me. Watch and wait with loving grief. I must bear the sins of all who live by Me.

The disciple of My heart, who drew his innocence and virgin purity from Me must learn the lesson that My body broken and My blood poured out are now the only food that can preserve from guilt and purify for heaven.

While I lie so helpless in the agonies of fear there is another night I feel, whose shadows only touch Me now. I shall feel the sins of all mankind; and as I sink to die, when utter weakness comes, the sword of Heaven shall smite Me in My tenderest point. The consoling presence of My Father and the Spirit consubstantial shall forsake Me when I need it most. Dost thou wonder that I fear, when before My fainting eyes and trembling heart this chasm opens wide to close Me in its awful depths? Already do I seem to feel the pains of death. Already do I see the tomb wherein My cold and lifeless body shall be laid. There shall I rest as humbled and as prostrate as if I were not God.

Now, My child, to whom I open thus the secrets of My agony, canst thou stay and watch with Me? Canst thou bear the shadows where I tremble so? Where My soul is filled with horror and My fear is like to death, canst thou come with Me? Thou canst never know what I have borne. I love thee far too much to break thy heart. And yet I yearn to bring thee to My close embrace, and be with thee as is the lover with the loved. I yearn to put My hand upon thy wounds, to chase the shadows from thy sky, to wash thee pure from every stain, to make thee like the crystal mirror that sends back My light. I would have thee for My own, where no shade can come between thee and My love. I thought of thee when in Gethsemani I lay so agonized with fear. I have often feared for thee. I feared to lose thee. Thou didst wear My ring upon thy hand, and thou didst call Me Bridegroom, too. Yet with tears I watched thee when I saw thee turn to creature love or rejoice in anything save Me. I have followed thee when thou wast forgetting Me and all thy love was not My own. Thou didst make Me fear in the garden even of My woe. But now I hold thee fast. If thou wilt not fear to stay with Me, the horror that I felt shall be thy cure. What I have borne shall not prevail against thee. Watch and pray, and love Me, too, with all thy heart. I am thy God. What can harm thee when I am near? Thy fear shall bind thee to My heart, and the brighter shall ascend thy love.

Dearest Lord, I thank Thee for these words. I tremble as I feel the shadows which so darkly covered Thee. I will watch with Thee. I will never leave Thy side. I could not live if there were parting now. I am not brave. I know how weak I am when danger threatens or the icy waters chill my blood. I promise nothing but to follow Thee. Let my days be dark, my nights a vigil endless, if so I closely cling to Thee. Yet I beg Thee to prepare my way. Let my heart be Thine, and when the path grows drear and sight is gone, when I can hardly feel, I know that Thou art near. Jesus, O my only Love! I watch and wait for Thee. My faith can never fail; and if the darkness seem too great, and mighty waves encompass me, my grateful heart shall hold its love, my voice shall sound Thy dearest name. Above the waters in their rage, above the forms of ill, the phantoms of the night, the spectres of my sins, one word shall still my fears, one word shall sound above the storms.

Jesus, Lord, my love above the depths ascends to Thee; I watch. I wait for Thee.

MEDITATION THIRD.

THE AGONY OF LONELINESS.

MEDITATION THIRD.

THE AGONY OF LONELINESS.

"He hath led Me and brought Me into darkness, and not into light. He hath set Me in the dark places, as those that are dead for ever. Yea, and when I cry, and entreat, He hath shut out my prayer."—LAMENTATIONS iii. 2, 6, 8.

CANST thou watch with Me? It will be little for thy love to do, if I am at thy side, and My hand shall hold thee up. Dost thou love me well enough to watch when I shall lead thee into darkness where no light is seen, to the places drear where I shall hide thee all alone and then withdraw My consolations? If I shall shut out thy prayer, and seem to go away for ever; if I let the tempter come to tell thee I am gone, to bid thee know I love thee not, that I have given thee to outer darkness, that thou art no longer Mine; art thou brave enough to wait in hope? When faith becomes thine only strength, and phantom forms are crowding round thee, and unearthly voices laugh to scorn thy confidence, wilt thou then abide? Canst thou, the lover of My bleeding heart, abide in seeming exile and bear something of My agony of loneliness? Listen, then, and I will tell thee, as I may, how I suffered in the garden shades when I was left alone. If it be hard for thee to bear the faintest shadow of My woe, what thinkest thou of My sad desolation when, as God, I stripped Myself of every light, and bade the creature, animate and inanimate, depart, and even hid the rays of My eternal glory, throwing densest clouds between the heavenly throne and My agonizing soul?

If I tell thee something of my loneliness, perhaps the thought may cheer thee when thy trial comes. The memory of this awful night, the picture of My prostrate, bleeding form, may give thee constancy, may make thee even love to be alone for Me, may help thee in thy promise to abide and watch with Me.

When I went down to My Gethsemani I willed to be alone. I willed to suffer, and from My bed of agony I shut out created love; and even of the fire that burned so brightly in few faithful hearts, even of the love divine of the Father and the Spirit, I made a torture, for I barred it out. When God made man willeth desolation, can any finite spirit sound its depths?

The love of the inanimate creation came not near Me in that hour. The earth put on a sable pall and seemed to cast Me from its bosom. It trembled as I touched it, as if some horror had possessed its depths. The voice of warning came from caverns of the sea; from the caves within the mountains on whose threatening brow the frown of anger seemed to settle down. The trees stood still and drooped their sorrowing branches, as if there were no life to move them now, as if cold death had seized them in their prime. It was not winter's frost, it was not decay, but sudden stoppage of the power of life. The flowers, whose smile was ever sweet, now fell as withered on their stems as if some palsied hand had crushed them in its grasp. The light rejoicing in My presence, and imaging to created things My glory, seemed extinguished. "The sun was turned to darkness, and the moon to blood." The stars were hidden in the vault of heaven, as if there were no light, as if the night of chaos had renewed its reign of horror.

The ranks of myriad life retreated from

the exiled Son of God. The beasts were hidden in their dens, appalled with fear. The birds, whose tuneful song exults in light, were nestling in the forest shades, as if the terror of some mighty power had struck them dumb. Upon the darkness piled around Me as a solid mass no hum of insect life arose to tell me that a living thing was moving near Me. I was hidden in the caverns drear of that which seemed a universal death. Down, down I sank as if to endless depths, where billows of the mighty ocean rolled above Me. The angels of My court, who always watched around My steps, were bidden to depart. I would not let them come within my living sepulchre. Unwillingly did they retreat, and stood with drooping wings beyond the clouds that covered Me. The valiant prince who leads the armies of My Father bowed his head and sheathed his sword. And Gabriel, guardian of

My Mother and of My humanity, passed away with trembling voice, while Raphael had no place within the garden where his King lay bleeding. I shut out their loving hearts, the blessed peace of their intelligence, and even would not think of seraph voices raised in adoration pure, nor hear the notes of their celestial song. I bade them stand in silence. Even in high heaven I hushed the canticles of joy.

And of those whom I redeemed, the men whose nature I had taken, the fellows of My race, there were none to comfort Me. The few whose hearts were aching for Me were away, shut out by My own will. My Blessed Mother would have come, but I loved her far too much to bring her here. I could not crucify her soul before the time, and so I saw her in her agony as far from me she watched and prayed. I would not think of her within this awful hour, for her anguish filled My cup, and as I drank it down how could her breaking heart console me? If she had seen My sweat of blood and touched My agonizing head, or knelt beside Me on the ground, she might have fallen crushed. She might have died beside Me, and the angels would have rushed unbidden to her aid. I could not have held them back. No! I felt her fearful woe, the anguish of her precious soul; I would not let her touch this chalice. I would drink it all alone.

I called for My disciples, and I begged them to remain with Me. Some fearful gloom appalled them, and the sadness of the day had wearied them. The baptism of their blood could not precede the Pentecostal flood of fire. The traitor was hastening on his way to seize Me for Mine enemies, to betray Me with his kiss. The eleven were overcome with sleep. They had heard Me warn them of approaching death. They had feasted on the body and the blood which on the morrow should be shed. And yet far away from Me, as if forgetting all My sorrows, they were sleeping. I took the three apostles whom I led to Thabor's height to see My glory. I asked them to draw nearer to My great humiliation, to see how low the Son of God could lie. They were so dear to Me I did not fear to try them in My lonely hour of woe. Even *they* could sleep. I saw the unconscious form of James, the heavy eyes of Peter, and even the exhausted face of John. Three times I begged them with My tears to wake and speak to Me. I could not rouse them from their sleep.

And yet, had they waked, what consolation could they bring, when I was bleeding for them, feeling all their future suffering, their fires of martyrdom; and when My strength was failing that I might give it all to them? They could have offered Me their sympathy when I was so forsaken and so sad. It might have added to the burden which was crushing Me, to see their tears; and yet the offering had been grateful to My love.

I read the souls of men—those who kill Me on the morrow, those who called Me friend, from whose hearts or homes I chased the gloom of sorrow or of sin. There was no comfort in the sight. There was hypocrisy, a false profession, or a selfish love. They loved Me for My benefits. Few love Me for Myself. This sight but added to My loneliness, and so I closed My eyes and bowed My head upon the ground, which, if it feared Me in My sorrow, did not hate Me, did not deceive Me with false words. I even kissed the grass so moistened with My blood, that it gave Me shelter in My grief and did not refuse Me rest or rudely cast aside My tears.

To make My desolation full of bitterness the evil spirits crowded round Me, and I bade them come. Their chains were loosed to do their worst against Me, to torment Me with their scorn, to oppress My soul with their malignant hate. Their movements were appalling to My every sense; their breath was baneful, their words were wounding to My honor, and their fiery eyes were flashing on Me like the meteors of the night. I was not in hell, and yet the flames of hell were burning in their hearts, and the smoke of fires eternal filled the heavily laden air. I was worse than exiles far from home, with enemies around Me; and the awful loneliness of spirits lost was weighing on Me. I, the Son of God, the brightness of the Father's face, by all created things deserted, save only by the powers of hell, exulting in their hour of seeming victory.

I have a deeper anguish now to tell thee of. I know not if thy mind canst understand My words. If thou art My child lift up thy voice and pray. Close thine eyes to all created sights, thine ears to all created sounds, and listen while the Eternal Spirit prays with thee. My Father then withdrew from Me the smile which ever held Me up in all My great humiliations. I saw His face as on it mantled the dread clouds of vengeance. He drew the sword divine to smite Me as if I were not His Son. He turned from Me as if His anger kindled at My sight and were to spend itself on Me, so helpless and so crushed. I cried, "Father, Father, is it Thou? Is this the tempest of Thy wrath to break on Thy co-equal Son?" I could not see, for blindness overcame Me, and I fell as one dead. There was no relenting then. Upon

My breaking heart, My bleeding form, the everlasting sword came down. Oh! it has power to pierce, to slay, to separate the soul from its material frame, to crush the body, and to penetrate the springs of life and thought.

I looked upward to the throne where amid the Cherubim am I adored. A night of more than mortal gloom hung between Me and the sceptre of My everlasting reign. The Paraclete proceeding from Me in the eternal act of love had hid His face, and desolation drear was sinking on My soul, then struggling for the breath of life. No rays of mercy came; no beams of warmth to cheer My freezing heart. The Spirit held the clouds of wrath between Me and the throne. I bore the weight of justice fierce proceeding from the sanctity of God. For sinners was I dying, and with sinners I must take My place, and in My agonizing soul and crushed humanity bear their punishment, and as the chief of criminals must feel the hatred of the Infinite for sin.

And with the Father and the Holy Ghost My will moved freely in that awful night. I wrought with them their work of wrath on Me. I put from My humanity, in this direst hour, the consoling rays of My divinity, and as God I plunged My manhood in the depths of gloom. My Godhead's cheering power I turned, that it should magnify My deep humiliation; and the voice of My divinity but told Me of the wrath divine, and made Me feel, as none but God could feel, the wounds inflicted by His hand upon the body and the soul in union everlasting with the person of the Word. The great humiliation of God's Son could be measured by the Infinite alone. So while consolation could not come, I bowed Myself beneath the lash of vengeance, and, with the Father and the Holy Ghost, I moved upon the waste of woe and plunged beneath the depths of wrath, that I might be indeed alone. And here, My child, My words must cease. I can speak no more. God alone can follow Me within the awful caverns of the deep. This agony of loneliness is far beyond the reach of intelligence created. Even love redeemed, love springing from My bleeding heart, love formed and nurtured in My breast, can never pierce these clouds nor be with Me within this veil where I, as God, descend to suffer and to bear the burden of the world's offence against the majesty divine. Thy love would bid thee dare to follow Me; but it were vain to try. Where angels cannot come, where My spotless Mother stands in awe, where the thunders of a broken law and terrors of avenging Deity are voices from the throne, the child so near My heart must kneel away, or only touch the outline of the distant cloud.

And yet I love thy sympathy. I yearn for perfect union with thee. My tenderness for thee is far above thy sight. Come close to Me and follow Me with fear. I am a jealous lover, reading all thy thoughts. If I call thee to the shadows of Gethsemani, if there I leave thee all alone, it is the proof of My espousals. There before the day shall dawn, before the nuptial joys be thine, I teach thee of thy spouse. I open to thy love the wonders of My grace. I purify thee from the stains of every sin. I empty thee of self. I teach thee thine own nothingness, and make the night profound, until I come alone with morning beams to claim thee as My own, to press thee to My breast, to tell thee of the crown prepared for thee. From loneliness there cometh joy. My saints shall welcome thee;

the fulness of My love shall fill thee with the bliss of heaven. Take courage, then, if thou art lonely; know that I am leading thee. I prove thy faith. "Canst thou stay one hour and watch with Me?" If I break the ties of earth and take from thee the bonds that bind thee to the creature; if I make of thine affections sources strong and deep of sorrow; if all that thou couldst lean upon shall fall beneath thee, and the silent grave shall bury all thy loves, canst thou bear the desolation? Art thou willing to be alone with Me? If the voice that led thee to My arms, and taught thee of the treasures hid in Me, is stilled within the tomb; if there are none around thee that can feel the meaning of thy words and deeds; if the gentleness of sympathy be turned to cold indifference, and for wasted strength and love there come ingratitude; and the waters that were sweet be turned to bitterness, wilt thou repine or murmur at My ways with thee? If even from the sanctuary I expel the light, and darkness shrouds the blessings of My sacramental throne; if even when I give Myself to thee in highest acts of love thy heart is heavy, and desolation dwells where faith alone lifts up its light; if thou canst not raise one thought of home, and seemest far from Mine embrace, an exile from the sweetness thou hast known, and callest to thy side in vain the saints who once protected thee, or angels of My court with whom thou once didst live; wilt thou complain or think Me cruel to thee? If I do more than this, and seem to leave thee as if I loved thee not, go far away when loneliness has reached its height, and let thee weep and yearn for Me; canst thou then abide in faith? Will the waters of thy desert chill thy love, and wilt thou turn away and count the cost of thine espousals to a King who crucified Himself to reign in bleeding hearts? Wilt thou cry: "Dearest Lord, I came to watch with Thee; I promised to abide for ever at Thy side, and for Thy love I have forsaken all; I have naught but Thee, and now Thou leavest me! I did not promise to abide alone, I cannot bear the night where Thou art not. My heart will break, and I shall die of loneliness. I was watching with Thee, and now I am in dreariness to die, watching I know not what, I know not where, in places desolate where I can neither see, nor hear, nor feel"? Shall this be all thy courage now, when once thy heart did seek to go within the Olive shades and ask to follow Me? Dost thou only walk by sight? Must thou see and hear to know that I am near? Thou didst leave all, but didst thou leave thyself? Wilt thou direct

Me in the ways I lead, or think that I am not within the cloud? It were well to realize that I am God, that I alone must reign, that in the souls I gather to My heart My will must rule omnipotent. In these deep shades self-will shall die and I will prove thy faith. Is it My grace thou seekest, or is it Me?

By the pain of seeming parting, by the dreariness of exile, I am washing out thy stains. I cannot lift thee to My side and before My saints espouse thee until thy heart is dead to all but Me, until thou canst not will the light, the rest from pain, the consolations of My face, if I thy Master choose for thee the night. Thou must put thy hands in Mine and ask for nothing but My will. In this Gethsemani thy pride shall fall for ever, thy subtle love of self, the vain complacency that counts My gifts as if they were thine own, and takes for courage and heroic love the sweetness that I grant to draw thee to the death that comes before the dawn, the morning of the new life. If thou art taken at thy word, wilt thou repine? If the Olive shades are dark beyond thy thought; then remember Me when so desolate I lay upon the crimsoned turf, thy God in utter loneliness, whose aching heart sent forth its blood from every pore; when night divine o'erwhelmed Me, and I cried: "O Father! must I drink this cup? Not My will but Thine be done." No night like Mine shall fall upon thee. No cup like Mine shall touch thy lips. Believe Me, I will never leave thee. In the thickest darkness I am nearest thee; and when thy loneliness seems worse than death I am unseen beside thee, watching well thine every thought, coming closer to thy side, proving to My Father and His saints thy constancy. The shadows chase the shadows, and the clouds dispel the gloom. The darkness that I send casts out the shades of earth, and the natural shall flee before the touch of God. Where nature dies there I shall live. If thou hast faith and wilt abide and learn to love the ways of grace, I teach thee lessons which the fearful never know. I can reveal Myself to thee and show thy yearning love the depths of tenderness within My breast. I can embrace thee. I can love thee as I will. I can put My heart in thine, and thine in Mine. Only fear not in the cloud; thou dost not see, but I am looking in thy face; thou dost not feel, but I am holding fast thy hands; thou dost not hear My voice, but I am speaking of thy love in sweetest tones unto My Father and the Spirit. I am telling to the angel choirs of nuptials that shall come, and bidding them prepare the festal joys. They are watching in the lonely gloom; they wait to comfort thee when morning dawns. I never loved thee more. I see thee true to Me in thy Gethsemani, and now I know thy heart is Mine. Blessed death to self and sense, that leads to life with Me. Blessed agony of loneliness, that opens wide the door of heaven, that leads thee to the company of saints, the home where loving arms of God shall hold thee fast for ever. There the nuptial chant shall sound, the shadows melt in uncreated light, and above the swelling song be heard the voices of the Bridegroom and the Bride.

Meditation Fourth.

THE AGONY OF SADNESS.

MEDITATION FOURTH.

THE AGONY OF SADNESS.

"My soul is sorrowful, even unto death."—St. Matthew xxvi. 38.

I AM listening, dearest Lord; the tender tones have moved me so that I am full of grief. Some shadows of Thy loneliness oppress me, that my tears are prayers. The night is full of gloom; but I am watching near Thee, and I love Thee so because Thy words reveal to me Thyself. Thou dost speak to one like me, as lover to his friend. Oh! so precious are these treasures of Thine hours of grief. Thou hast called me child, and opened to my longing love Thine heart so infinitely sweet. Thou hast called me to Thy side and bidden me to stay.

I feel Thine agony, but I know not what it is. I feel *Thee*, and only Thee. All else is gone. I hardly know myself, who I am, or whence I come. The earth itself seems far away. I know not if there be a sun, or if the stars that gild the firmament are moving in their courses. I have forgotten creatures; and the faces I have known are strange to me. I have no memory; I have no past; I have no future. One thing I know—my Jesus in His agony is here. I see only *Him;* I hear His voice alone. I feel naught but Him. All is Jesus, and Jesus is my All.

And now an awful fear comes over me. My blessed Love is suffering more. He has not told me all. He lies more prostrate on the ground. He moves convulsively with pain. The blood is gushing in new torrents from His face and hands. Dearest Master, the midnight of Thy woe is not yet come. Thou art more sad. There is a heavier weight upon Thy breast, and Thy dear face betrays an awful struggle in Thy heart. I see deep dejection and a sadness overwhelming Thee. There is one expression in Thy prostrate form, in Thy hands and limbs and feet, in Thy royal head which lies so low. It is the language of a broken heart. O my Jesus! is there none to comfort Thee; is there no ray of joy to pierce this gloom; no memory that can rest Thy soul; no sight to soothe the anguish of Thy blood-stained eyes? One voice comes up to me. Thou dost not speak, and yet I hear. I feel the words that rise to me as from the crimsoned ground Thy lips are moving to the cry of sadness inexpressible. "My soul is tasting sorrow to its most awful possibility. It is like to death; it is worse than death.

If I were not God I should now die with agony."

Dearest Master, may I speak? May Thy loving though unworthy child draw near Thee in this hour? Canst Thou tell me of this sadness overwhelming Thee? May one like me dare look within the deeps that seem to swallow Thee and from Thy soul divine shut out the rays of light? I know I cannot follow Thee, nor ever penetrate the caverns drear where God alone descends; but may I hear a little of Thy woe? If my sympathy could reach Thee now, it seems that I would offer Thee my life. Yet I dare not say one word, I am so weak, inconstant, and so fearful in the face of danger. Oh! let my weakness cry to Thee; only let me love Thee, and I will ask no more.

Then there was silence like the utter death of sound. There was not a movement that could tell me there was life. It might have been an hour; it seemed an age. I could plead no more. In the stillness deep I neither moved a limb or feature. I hardly thought. My Master was in close communion with me, and I *felt* these words, which seemed to be within me and yet to come from Him. There was an awful nearness to my Love, while shadows of His heart encompassed me until I seemed to lose my life in His.

Child, whom I have called to watch with Me, whose love hath ventured here within the shades whence even angels fled, dost thou see Me sinking, sinking far away from thee? Wouldst thou know the sadness that prostrates Me now? Wouldst thou see the drops which from my chalice I am drinking here? I know not if My struggling soul can speak to thee as in grief intense it poureth out its life and sinks beneath a flood of woe. I am sad: there is no other word. Hast thou known sorrow? Have the ties which bound thy heart been snapped in twain? Has earth been desolate to thee? Has the created light seemed ever mockery to increase thy darkness? Hast thou been laid beneath a cross whose weight was crushing thee, till joy seemed dead before the open grave of all thy hopes? This is grief, perhaps; but *sadness* shows a deeper pang. Indeed a grave is here; the springs of life are quenched, decay is reigning in its blight; where phantom faces mock the tears that fall, and cruel voices tell of hopes extinguished, of loves departed, buried where no morning comes. Around, above, beneath is blackness; while on the heart there lies a weight no power can raise. It is crushing down; and with it life and hope and joy are sinking in the deep abyss. The tears would fall. The heart would struggle with convulsive sobs; the breast would pant for breath. But what are signs like these? They are the language of a wrestling with our woe. That sadness is the deepest where the avenues of sense seem turned to stone, and our intelligence is dumb, as if a prisoner in a living tomb.

Have I told thee of a sadness thou hast known? Have I touched the strings whose quick response reveals the memory of anguish known to God, of which thou hast no words? Then let remembrance help thee to the knowledge of My grief. Thou hast suffered as a creature. I have suffered as a God. Thy heart is finite and hath known the taint of sin. My heart is God's, the resting-place of His great tenderness, the home of love divine. Its birthright is the Father's face with all the bliss of deity. The rays that shine within it are the light that dwells upon the throne.

If the sadness crushes thee, what must that awful sorrow be which prostrates thy God, and weighs Him down until His mighty arm seems paralyzed, and the Creator weeps and struggles with a sweat of blood?

I cannot tell thee of the drops within the chalice of My agony. To the Father and the Spirit My broken heart is open. It rises to the pity and the justice of the Deity. I tell thee all I may, and even more than thou canst understand. Pray the mighty Spirit to inspire thee, to touch the powers of thine intelligence, and in the future days to bring these precious revelations to thy loving memory.

I was bending under the dread hand of God. I was the Lamb of sacrifice. The cruel death before Me was My choice. The knife was in the Father's hand to slay His Son. He could not shrink back nor fail to make the work complete. This was the moment of the ages. The hour had come. The Lamb was ready and His breast was bared. No wonder that the Lamb was desolate, led out to slaughter, none to pity, none to spare. But that the knife might find Him ready, and go down to pierce the tenderest heart, the face of God must be averted and anger dwell where love eternal sprang. He was as if the sinner in whose place He stood. The justice of the Trinity beheld Him not as the co equal Word. Sins clothed Him as a garment then—the sins of every age, of every heart. The sins of every sense and limb crept over Him, like noisome reptiles turning round, until they hid His face, and He seemed to see but sin, to hear but sin, to taste but sin, to feel but sin. No crime too vile to come and lay its weight upon Him now! The days before the flood were here; the days of

Sodom and Gomorrah; the days of base idolatry, when vice itself was made a god; the days of Israel's fall and final ruin; the days of heresy and separation from the ark of God, His body mystical. Sins of the intelligence and will, crimes that called to Heaven for vengeance, vices of the passions in their dark pollution—all were laid on Him, and as a filthy robe were wound around Him. He could hardly recognize His limbs and senses as the members of the incarnate Son. And with their drear pollution and the crimson stream of guilt there came the wretchedness of wasted grace, the stings of deep remorse, the tortures of the undying worm. The miseries of broken hearts, the death of souls, the dire corruption of the grave where sin in all its foulness reigns, were all upon Him. Where He had made an Eden fair, there came an earth defiled, the vale of sorrow and the home of bitterness. No crime of thought, or word, or hand, or deed which did not bear its weight on Him. All sins and griefs of man were burdens of His heart. Wonderest thou that He lay prostrate and could scarcely rise beneath the load?

I am speaking of Myself; for as I looked upon My body crushed and soul afflicted, I seemed as if another, the victim of My love for God, standing in the persons of the sinners vile whose wounds I bore, bruised and marred and all unlike the brightness of the Father's image. So spoke the Spirit as the eternal Three in One beheld this scene, and the Lamb in helplessness before them.

"Who can believe the fearful story? To whom is known the arm of God, the Consubstantial Word? There is no beauty here, nor comeliness. We have seen him, and, alas! there was no sightliness. Who would desire Him? Despised of all, He is of men the most abject. Sorrows and infirmity are all His daily life. He hath the look of one contemned; who could esteem Him? He wears the face and form of lepers struck by God and heavily afflicted. His wounds are wounds of others' sins; His bruises are the blows of others' crimes; He is bearing punishment for man's iniquities, while on His bleeding heart is laid the weight of all transgression. It was His will to be the sacrifice. The Lamb of God lies dumb, and unresistingly is led to slaughter." *

My child, for whom I suffered so, I would that I could tell thee of this agony while thus the burden of the world's transgressions crushed Me to the earth. God alone can feel the depth of My humiliation. The Infinite alone can know the shame and guilt of sin, and tremble at its awful nearness. And in My grief I

* Isaias liii. 1-7.

seemed to touch the lowest and the vilest, souls I could not save, who only mocked My sweat of blood and called Me weak, or in their derision laughed that God should suffer or become a victim sacrificed by His own will, when, without the pangs of death, He might have saved the sinner if He would. Hell with lurid flames arose before Mine eyes; the sinless lake of pain was near Me. I wrestled with the demons in their frantic rage, and spirits lost were jeering at My useless woe.

I felt the sins of Mine elect, the weakness of My saints, the guilt of those I love, for whom My heart was giving out its blood. Had I not bowed so low, had I not touched the chalice, where had been the throng of virgins and the white-robed army of the martyrs? How in darkest places of the earth could purity have gleamed or innocence have lifted up its torch? How could the stain of crime be washed away, and Eden come again to new-born souls? Alas! My blood must flow; and that it gain full power to cleanse the vile, and turn the springs polluted into founts of life and light, My heart must send it forth with all the vigor of a God. And now, My loving child, fear not, do not despair. I will tell thee how I bore *thy* sins; how every thought and word and deed of thine inconstancy to Me were like the poisoned spears to wound Me in My tenderest point, to touch the fountains of My love for thee, to press upon the veins of thy Beloved and make them bleed! Yes, I wept for thee. Thou wast not always wholly Mine. And if I had not suffered to this sweat of blood, how could I have brought thee back from wanderings strange and creature snares, and laid thee on My shoulders bare and bruised, and then have looked thee in the face with tearful eyes; have made thee love Me, and have taught thee what I am, the sweetness of My heart? Weep, my child; here let thy tears run down with Mine. It needed this Gethsemani to win thee to My side. Behold Me here so low, so sad, for thee. I am prostrate here that thou mayest rise, with thy lamps new lighted, ready for the nuptial rite, the hour of thine espousals to a bleeding King. So gladly I this burden bear, and even pray the bitter waters to submerge Me in their depths; I touch the limits of a sadness reaching far beyond the bounds of things created, that I may make thee glad in that new life which springeth from the fountains of My blood.

And while I lay beneath this burden of the world's transgression, of every human misery, of every grief that man can know, I looked upon My humanity and trembled at the sight. This greatest work of God, this body framed of

Mary's virgin blood, this soul resplendent with the light of deity—where were they now? Where was the brightness of the Father's image; where the beauty which had ravished all the angel choirs; where the might of God's right Arm; where the power of the unconquerable Word? So ill My visage seemed, so bruised My form, that I was hardly man; much less did I appear as God. Oh! it filled My soul with sadness crushing all My life to look upon Myself and feel the depth to which God's only Son had sunk. I was indeed despised, cast out by man, a leper bending 'neath the wrath of heaven. The sight appalled the Cherubim and Seraphim, whose tearful eyes were turned away. They looked from My humiliation to the throne. The cloud had passed before them. The uncreated rays were hid. There was no word to tell them why their King lay thus, His heavenly purple dragged in mire, without an angel for His guard, the most abject of all created things.

And then I drew Me to the hearts I love, the virgin souls whom I was making pure, the saints who followed Me within these awful shades and to the watch on Calvary. I saw their sins effaced, their stains made clean, their chains set free ;. I was bearing on My broken heart their burden drear, which never on their souls should fall ; I was bound, and they were free. And yet I could not keep the waters of affliction from them, nor hold back the spear that pierced Me through and through from touching them. It made Me sad to see them suffer so. I counted all their tears ; I treasured up their pains. They were the purchase of My cross. They suffered for My love, and where the hurt was deep and heart recoiled, they thought of Me and blessed the hour of their companionship with Jesus in the garden of His grief. I loved.

them so for their fidelity to Me in shadows dire where every creature help had failed. I saw their straining eyes, as with the tears of gratitude they searched for Me, and through the olive-trees their cry was heard: "Jesus, Master, let me come to Thee!" It was I, indeed, who suffered then, and in them endured.

The Martyrs in their crimson robes all passed before Me. I saw their pangs, the fearful fires, the cruel sword, the rack, the scourge, the nails. I felt their long and awful deaths, where angels with the crown of life were watching all their wrestlings with the torture, and palms of glory waited for them. While I lay there as if unconscious in My agony, My heart was giving them My strength, My fortitude was theirs, and I was drinking in my chalice sad the blood they shed for Me. I saw My loved ones in that hour, and every weight that ever rested on their hearts was bearing down on Me.

My apostles dear, so soon to die; My priests; confessors in their strength of faith—they passed before Me one by one. For each there was a tear, for each a portion in My woe.

I saw My Church, My body mystical, encompassed round with fire and sword, its long career the record of My griefs. I was its image as I lay there so low. There was the body of the Word, the Second Adam thus discomfited; the sacred tabernacle of the Lord, the ark of safety from the flood. No blows that struck the Church were half so fierce as those that rained on Me; no oppression of the home of God on earth was half so crushing as the weight which fell upon the eternal Son of God, as in Gethsemani He lay alone without a solace, desolate and sad, in battle where it seemed the arm of the Omnipotent had failed, and devils led their conquering hosts to trample on Him in His dire defeat.

There was another woe. And when I look upon it as it came to crush Me, I am so sad that I can hardly speak. You know a little of My love, a little of the depth divine of tenderness that dwells in Me; you know how dear to Me are souls whom I espouse, whose hearts I lead to nuptial joys and take within My glad embrace. Oh! what you know is little of the truth. I am sweetness infinite, love that hath no bounds, and when I clasp a soul within My arms, they are the mighty arms of God.

Could I tell you how I love My Mother blest, My priceless one, My dearest treasure in this vale of tears? Ah! I tell it not to angels listening in the wonder of their high intelligence. She far excels their brightness; and the rays that clothe her soul, proceeding from the throne, are telling to the Father and the Spirit of My love for her. The mighty Trinity bows down to hear the story, and the Three in One rejoice and call her Queen. Yet lift up thy heart, my child, and look beyond the powers of sense. I owe thee to My Mother; she hath prayed for thee. She brought thee to My side. Her blessed hands have led thee to My home. They held thee up when first I looked on thee and heard her say, "Behold my child and Thine." I know thou lovest her with all the tenderness I gave to thee. If I did not see thee in her arms, I could not be Thine. No child can find a place within My nuptial halls but those My Mother brings with her sweet smile. Then, from thy love to her, lift up thy soul and think what she must be to Me.

I saw her in this night of woe as in her home she knelt and watched and prayed. I saw her sighs, I heard her sobs, I felt the anguish of her heart. Her soul was near to Mine, never nearer than within this fearful hour. I looked upon her blessed face, and how I loved that face the Three in One alone can know. The eyes that ever sought My gaze with more than mother's love were red with tears. The lines of agony were written where the uncreated beauty dwelt. Her precious hands were pale and cold, and moved as if convulsively in prayer. She fell with Me, and when I fainted, she was prostrate too. I felt the beatings of her heart responsive to My grief: it panted for the breath of life. Oh! how I loved her then! My child, there are no words to tell my grief. I yearned to take her in My arms, to call her by her dearest name, to drive from her the clouds away, and lift the pall which covered her bright soul. Yet that dark pall could not be raised. She was My own, My Mother dear, with love for Me that reached the bounds of all created strength. When I must suffer, could I say to her, "Mother, think no more of Me; sorrow not when I am passing through My agony"? This had hurt her heart and wounded deep the tenderest feelings of her soul. She must be with Me in pain, for indeed our hearts are one. I could not bring her here. This were too much for her and Me. She feels the struggles of my soul; she feels the drops of blood as one by one they cover me with this My crimson robe. I would not let her *see* this sweat of blood, this awful weakness of her child. Enough has she to bear when I shall meet her on My way to Golgotha, the cross upon My shoulders, treading in My blood. Enough to follow Me to Calvary, to stand beneath Me when My dying hour shall come, and let My failing eyes drink in her parting look of love. Yet, oh! how sad I was to feel her woes! It almost killed Me to behold her grief. Down in the crimsoned ground I hid

Mine eyes, and sighed as if for death.
O cruel, cruel sin that crucifies a God
and must crucify the Mother too! My
child, my heart is broken now. I
say no more. I cannot speak. Oh!
leave Me with the earth on which I lie
alone. Here let Me weep and here give
out My blood. God knows My loneliness. To Him I need not speak.

And if you truly love your brokenhearted King, then speak no more. It
is the hour of silence, through the earth;
in heaven. Go kneel and pray. Never
can I break your heart as sin has broken Mine.

Meditation Fifth.

THE AGONY OF PAIN.

MEDITATION FIFTH.

THE AGONY OF PAIN.

"Tribulation is very near: there is none to help Me. I am poured out like water. My heart is become like wax melting in the midst of My bowels. My strength is dried up like a potsherd, and My tongue hath cleaved to my jaws, and Thou hast brought Me down to the dust of death. They have dug My hands and feet; they have numbered all my bones."—PSALM xxi. 12-17.

WHEN thus my Master ceased to speak, and begged for solitude to ease His grief, my soul was still. It was not alone the stillness of the senses. It was an awful stillness of my soul. I cannot tell of this, for it was not an earthly silence. My being seemed no more my own; and all my consciousness was lost in Him who, lying there, upheld me that I could be still. Did I pray? Tell me, angel guide, oh! was it prayer? I sent my heart to watch beside my prostrate Lord, and I was so sad that I cannot speak of it. Ah! sadness is no word. There is no word. There is a language deep which hath no signs. Bitter was the hour, too bitter far for utterance. One thing alone I knew: my Jesus was before me. My weeping Love was lying there. I felt *Him;* I had no other sense. I suffered, but I know not how. I dare not say it, yet I seemed to suffer there with Him. Could this be true for one like me? Did I really grieve with Him? Was I then so near to Him that He could make me partner of His woe?

Then, while I suffered so, and tears like rain ran down, and new affection for my dearest Lord was filling up my bursting heart, I was awakened to the sense of life. I looked before me, and the darkness was more dense. I put out my trembling hands, and, like one blind, I seemed to touch the cloud that as a wall surrounded me. My ears alone had life, and took the place of every other sense. From the earth there came a voice. I knew the tones. Even in their deathlike feebleness no tones but His could move me from that stillness where my lips seemed closed for ever.

O my Blessed Love! is it indeed Thy voice? And wilt Thou speak to me again? I know, I feel, Thy fearful agony has yet not reached its height. Canst Thou tell me more? If I may hear another word my grateful soul shall praise Thee in eternity. May I listen while the shadows deepen and the cloud is heavy on Thee? I would know all I can. I only ask for love, because Thou art so dear to me. Nearer am I to Thee now than I ever hoped to be. I fear I am too bold; and yet I bless these awful hours. Could I have known Thee in Thy depth of tenderness, if I had not known this darkness of Gethsemani?

Child of My sorrows, espoused to Me in blood, I love to speak to thee; I love to tell thee of the burden which I bear. I am bearing it for thee, and I am loving thee with every pain. Each sharp agony unites My soul to thine. Each awful pang but brings Me closer to thy heart, and gives Me right to fold thee to My breast. Let Me tell Thee of My pain. The cloud of sadness that oppressed My soul as if the bands of death had bound Me is here lifted up. I am suffering tortures new at every breath, and yet my heart is more at ease. I will reveal to thee an agony whose sharpness is relief from that depression darker than the night of chaos when the Spirit moved upon the void. I will lift up My aching head, and for a moment stay My tears. I tell thee how upon My broken form the shafts of anger fell, and lightnings of the wrath of God were playing on My nerves that I might suffer pain, and of the cup of torture drink the dregs. As I lay there I passed My passion through. I took up every pang. I anticipated all. I felt the cross, the scourge, the crown of thorns, the nail, the spear. I felt the blows upon My face, the spittle of the crowd, the angry curses of the mob. In My flesh, exhausted with the sweat of blood, I was mocked, and scourged, and crucified before the time.

Listen, child, and as thou art My own, thou wilt love to dwell upon My wounds, to study every pain, with deep affection linger as I shall each grief unfold, and open to thy sight the picture of a martyred God.

Didst thou know Thy Love was crucified, that thou art now His bride, that the marriage-bells were sounding in the garden, ringing loud on Calvary? Didst thou know that when He touched thy hand, and put on thee the wedding-ring, His fingers were so red with blood? Didst thou know that He was full of pain, and trembling with the pangs of mortal anguish, when He drew thee to His side and called thee His? Hereafter thou shalt know the whole; yet I will teach thee now the lesson that may serve thee in thy pangs, and when thy crosses come shall turn thine eyes to Me. I shall not ask My saints to bear what I have borne.. Look, then, with prayerful heart, and nerve thyself to see. Where I have fainted, and thy God was weak, canst thou look on and live?

Ah! hast thou known a pain severe, and full of death, making of the flesh one realm of torture, running through the veins, piercing nerves, dividing bones, and burning at the seat of life? There are bitter pangs, the punishments of crime; there are torments cruel rage hath found to sate its vengeance on the dying frame. There are martyrs for My faith treading in their paths of agony to find the likeness to My cross. I have taken all their pains. I have gone before to bless their anguish with My presence, and to track the way that leads to crowns eternal in the heavens.

Their strife was fierce, the struggle dire; yet am I their King, and far as earth from heaven their agonies from Mine. I am God, and in the realm of torture I am reigning. Without an equal have I suffered, and there is no cup of grief intense I have not tasted to the full. To the utmost power of pain have I mounted; to the depths of keenest agony I have gone down. And My nature, so divine, so sensitive to feel, hath strained its great capacities of suffering, that the soul and body of the Word might thus "exhaust the sins of many" and be perfect in its sacrifice. The pangs which I endured upon Me came in one assault. I bade them come together, and I bared My breast that they might do their worst. I held them fast and would not yield; I let them waste their strength and wrestle with Me, and I suffered only as I willed. When the torments reached their height, when to its fiercest limit I had tasted every pain, then with My hands I touched the chilling stream of death, and bowed down lifeless to their rage. And every pang I took I held without relief throughout long hours—the endless hours when moments, counted by My pains, were ages drear. I held them all like furnaces of fire burning fiercely to the dying breath. I was bruised with stunning blows. The marks were on My head and breast and swollen face. I kept the sting until the last. The ropes that bound Me tore Me by their cruel tension, as they dragged Me like a beast along the streets, among the stones that pierced My feet. The stricture of the ropes I felt around My waist, upon My breast, even when on Calvary; and the cross with My convulsions caused the cruel mark to redden with My blood.

Naked at the pillar did I stand while scourges ploughed My flesh. My shoulders were one bleeding wound. I kept the agony and took it to the end. Upon the cross I nourished it, and would not then permit one pang to cease, or fail to feel one blow. I would be scourged unto the last, and willed to see the mangled shoulders bleed. I put the heavy cross upon them, that the gaping wounds might open wide and reveal in death the burden I had borne.

I would not that My bones should break. This were not worthy of the Lamb of God. But I took a direr pain, and let My limbs be forced apart, and from their sockets let My bones be torn. And thus I hung on Calvary, and thus I died.

They tore the skin and flayed Me as they mocked Me, tearing off My garments from My bruised and mangled flesh. This was anguish as of fire. I trembled as I meekly bore it to the cross and held it till the end.

They put upon My royal head a crown of thorns. With its sharp points they pressed it through the tenderest nerves. Upon My temples and against the bone it crowded down. It tore My forehead, it obscured My sight, it opened up a fount of pain; My aching, lacerated head was wild with anguish too intense for life. I nourished all these pangs. I would not let them go. Not an instant did they cease. I kept My cruel crown and wore it till I died.

The deathlike faintness such as only comes from loss of blood I suffered from the garden till with parting breath I yielded to the awful agony. I was fainting all the time, just living as I willed, and holding on to tortures to exhaust their power. I was nearer death than life. Beneath the cross I staggered on, so weary that My weariness was worse than pain.

My heart seemed filled with fire, and its pulsations ran like light, till breath was anguish to Me; and then by turns it almost ceased to beat, and like the chilling ice it lay with stifling weight within My breast. Now I was burning, burning, as if some penetrating fire were running in My veins, as if a heat of more than human power were turning into vapor fierce the solid flesh and bone. Then I was chilled to death, freezing, aching with the cold, hanging naked on My wounds, and trembling as the nails that held Me seemed as icy bands to burn Me with their cold intense.

There came a hunger, not from lack of food alone, but from exhaustion awful in its pain, as nature craved relief. The thirst from faintness and from bleeding so profusely was a fearful pang. I even cried aloud from awful thirst consuming Me; and as My tongue was parched, with lips wide open panting for a breath, the souls for whom I died were ready with their mockery. Upon My lips, so dry and feverish, even cracked with thirst, they put their vinegar and gall. I was hungry and athirst until I willed to die, and, prostrate on the ground, My tears were mingled with My blood. I took these pains and held them to My breast as if My dearest treasures. They were the price of souls. With these I bought My lovers true ; and as I drew them with the strength of God, I blessed the agonies that made them Mine.

So in fondness all divine I touched the scourge so soon to tear My back. I kissed the ropes so soon to bind My limbs. I took up the nails, and, as if I looked at gems, I laid them on My heart. The hammer which the ruffian hand should drive them with was dear to Me. I looked upon My hands and feet, and marked the place where they should pierce Me with an endless wound. I saw the thorns, so sharp, so soon to rest upon My brow. I touched their points with tenderness. This was the crown of the celestial King, who reigns by blood, and wins the hearts of men by pain. And when upon My royal head I saw this crown, I gathered to My close embrace the virgin souls that only know their bleeding Spouse and never fear the thorns.

I put My fingers on the cross and measured well its height and breadth. This was the tree of life, for ages seen in prophecy, to bear the quickening fruit, the living bread. Its type was once in Paradise, where innocence and beauty reigned beneath the smile of God. From Eden it has come to Calvary, and by that sacred wood I shall redeem the world. I touched and blessed the holes already made to hold the spikes when they should nail My lacerated feet and hands.

With affection uncontrolled I took the spear which should transpierce My heart in death. With transports of a God I kissed it many times. Blessed spear, I cried as then My Father heard— blessed spear, that in the heart of love incarnate shall reveal the depths and unfold the mercy of the Crucified, opening up the wound that flows for ever with the tide of pardon and of grace. As Adam, sleeping in the noon of Eden, saw his bride, so from this gaping wound within My breast I saw My spouse proceed, My spotless Church, the throng of virgins and of saints whose robes were glistening in the uncreated light, the children of the Word made flesh. And thus I turned and looked upon Myself; in every nerve and sense I felt My crucifixion, and to the chalice of My mortal anguish put My lips. Was I God, so low, so agonized with pain? Had the Love Eternal of the Father and the Spirit come to this? A prostrate form, too weak to stand, too helpless to lie still, convulsed with agony, bleeding freely, all alone, without a wound! Yes, this is God! Here is the horror of the scene. Here is the source of pain. He does not die. He takes up every drop of anguish possible, is crucified before His time, because He is your God.

Now, My precious child, if to thee I tell this agony, it is that I may to thy soul unfold the depth of My great love for thee. I suffered so that I might teach thee many lessons—lessons thou must learn if thou wilt come so near Me as thy heart would wish, and really touch Me with thy hands, and lay thy head upon My breast, and feel the pressure of Mine arms, and even hope to taste the kisses of My lips. I would that I might speak to thee, as I cannot speak to all. I would that I might here reveal to thine enlightened mind a little of the wealth that dwells in Me, a little of the treasure that thy Jesus is. I am God, and yet I would be thine, as if thou wast My only love. Can you know the length and breadth, and depth and height, of mercy infinite?

My agony of pain was needed to the blessing of thy cross. I grieve to see thee suffer pain. I bore thy griefs upon My heart. Thy sorrows, too, were all n Mine. How can I lead thee after Me, and make thee like thy Master, if thou hast no cross? How purge thee from thy dross, and in thy senses heal the wounds of sin? How refine the founts of feeling at their source, and make thy limbs and members fit to touch My flesh, if there be no agony like Mine? How canst thou pay thy debt to justice as exacting as divine, and so be free to stand before Me where My angels are not clean, if there be no penance laid on thee? And so I go before thee with My staff and rod. I hold thee up while thus in mercy I chastise thee. It is thy loving Lord that deals the blows. They fall from bleeding hands; they come from pity infinite; they hurt Me too, and I am weeping with thee. I must hide My face when tears are falling fast, and make thee feel that I am angry with thee. When My heart is breaking to console thee I cannot listen to the plea. I am truest to thee in thy pain, which is My grief. Thou didst ask for purity. Thou didst pray for My embrace. Canst thou, then, descend within the Olive shades with Me, that I may lead thee to the inner life where I unveil the riches of My grace?

Thou shalt never know a garden agony like Mine. The faintest shadow of the night is all I ask for thee. It shall wrap thy soul in gloom. It shall hurt as God alone can hurt. My fingers all divine shall touch the aching wounds, and play upon them as a God. Then think of Me when thus thy hour shall come. Let not the tempter lure thee to despair. I am with thee, mightier, dearer far than when I send the beams of joy or fill thee with the sweetness of My face. Didst thou know the heart thou choosest is a wounded heart, that thorns surround My brow, that marks of nails are in My hands? They that seek to follow Me, that would be

Mine, that long to know Me well, must touch the spear and thorns and nails. For I am crucified, and crucified shall be to every soul that finds the joy of My embrace.

In pain I send there is a grace I cannot give thee with the smile of peace. There is a merit in the sorrow fierce that with discerning love I mete to thee. It is thy cross. It is thy share of Calvary. It is thy burial from earth. It is the night before the dawn; the tomb that opens to a glorious life. Faint not, My child. Thou didst profess to love Me unto death. If thy pang be fierce, thy agony severe, it is My greatest gift to thee. Then in thine anguish think of Me. Remember when in awful night I lay upon the crimsoned ground and sighed My life away for thee. Unite thy pains to Mine. They are well known to Me. I bore them all, and blessed them with

My tears. Thou didst ask to suffer with
Me in the transports of thy love. Then
suffer as I will. Thine agony of pain
can never crush thy soul. Offer all for
Me. And I will come, though thou
shouldst never see My hands; I will
hold thy head and soothe thine aching
heart. Each pang I sanctify with gentleness
divine. I come with pain to those
I love. I am a sword to sever, and a
fire to burn. Each sorrow is a step that
leads within My home; each grief the
messenger of grace, guiding to a truer
nearness to thy heavenly Love. I am
winning thee, detaching thee from earth,
and clothing thee in bridal raiment for
thy King. Watch and wait, and tremble
not. Listen in thy grief. The marriage-
bells are sounding in thine ears. The
Bridegroom dear is coming with His train.
Celestial music falls from angel harps;
their choirs are singing welcome to the
bride.

Thine hour of death shall be thine hour of joy, when from thy bed of pain I lift thee up, to show to thee My face, to tell thee of My love, that I have loved thee long, that I will love thee to eternity.

MEDITATION SIXTH.

THE AGONY OF A WOUNDED HEART.

MEDITATION SIXTH.

THE AGONY OF A WOUNDED HEART.

"And they shall say to Him: What are these wounds in Thy hands? And He shall say: With these was I wounded in the house of them that loved Me."—ZACHARIAS xiii. 6.

WHEN my blessed Master spoke these joyous words my soul entranced seemed lost in Him. For a moment I forgot the fearful gloom which so encompassed me. My darkness seemed to turn to light, and far away my prayers were travelling to the land of peace, where tears and sorrow are unknown. I looked above me; through the parting clouds I saw the paradise of God, where 'mid the lilies, by the banks of crystal streams, the heavenly Shepherd leads His flock. Angels in their bright array were there, and virgin souls were kneeling round the King. My agony of pain was turned to ecstasy; the wounds the bleeding fingers touched were rays of light. I saw the ladder there as from the earth it reached to heaven. I saw the saints ascending to the throne. Upon the throne I saw the form of my Beloved; with grace and majesty He sat; the splendor of His face was brighter than the sun in his meridian strength. For a moment I forgot the garden where He suffered so, and I knew not the place in which I was nor where His love would guide me. When He is near I take no thought of time nor place. And He had lifted me away from earth. I seemed to lean upon His breast, all pain and danger past; to look with love into His blessed eyes; to see the glory of His smile, and feel the pressure of His arms. O my Beloved!

how can I thank Thee for this grace! How dear Thou art to me! Thy sweetness melts my soul. I am not living now, for Thou indeed art living in me. Blessed life to live in Him! One heart, one will, one joy! Only Jesus! There is nothing else. My very being cries with bliss, and speaks at every breath His precious name.

How long my ecstasy endured I cannot tell. Can angels count the moments of their blissful life before the King? I had travelled far, and I was blest indeed. It seemed no shadow could approach the home where with my Jesus I was feasting on His face. Had I forgot the Olive shades, the trembling form of my Beloved, the piteous cries, the sweat of blood? I had not forgotten *Him;* and yet He seemed to cast aside His crimson robe. I saw no tears upon His cheeks. His eyes so dear were full of smiles. Now suddenly there came a change—an awful change. From my brief joy there came a new and fearful grief. The light was gone. The gloom was deeper than before. The cold of icy winter chilled me through. I tried to see: my sight had gone. I tried to feel: there was no sense to guide my hands or feet. An awful pain was seizing on my heart; and in the night, so dense that every pulse was stilled, I heard a piteous cry. Oh! I have never heard a cry like that! Agony, as that of God, took voice, and there came upon the deep a wail of sorrow which unnerved me till I prayed for death. It is the angel of the grave that wraps his wings around my life; I feel the touch of his cold pinions and the darkness of the tomb! No, I am not dead! I yet can hear. I hear my Master dear. I cannot err. I know His voice. Oh! art Thou suffering more, my blessed Love? Couldst Thou suffer more? Hadst Thou not reached the height of pain? Only now Thy tones were not so full of tears. There was a trembling in Thy voice, as if the agony were breaking and the clouds that covered Thee were slowly passing on their way. What hath happened Thee? O my Master! speak to me once more. What new grief hath come to crush Thee in Thy weakness now?

He did not reply. I waited long. I prayed with all my soul. I begged for strength. I wept until my eyes were blind, and then I sobbed as if my heart would break. In this awful stillness, where I strained my hearing till it seemed that sense would cease, I heard again that piteous wail. O spirits of the light! oh! may I call you to this gloom? Can you help me hear these sorrowing tones, and live? Ah, hark! let not a pinion move; let not a breath from earth or heaven disturb me now. Oh!

He is crying to the Father, not to me. And will the Father hear? "Father, Father! must I drink this cup? Is there no relief? Could I be spared this torment of My wounded heart? Oh! must it be? Must I take this chalice drear? I am broken now with grief. Is this Thy will? I feel the agony will kill Me with its awful pain."

Then there came a pause. I heard the sound of sighs that pierced me like a thousand arrows in my flesh, and sobs so weak, and yet so pitiful, that in my fear I struggled hard to move, while seeming bands of ice were holding me like bars of iron in their mighty grasp. I could not move a limb or sense. Surely my heart is ceasing now to beat, I cried; the hour is come. Oh! where is my Beloved? Shall I go and thus bid *Him* farewell?

Listen once again. He speaks: "Father, Thy will be done. It thus must be. I take the cup. My hands are trembling so I cannot hold it to My mouth. Take Thou the chalice that I dread, and with Thy hands divine uplift it to My lips. My heart is wounded to the death—wounded as the Son of God alone could be—and yet I take it all. Oh! spare Me not. There is no more. When I have taken up the dregs of this My fearful cup, there is no more that I can do! Prostrate on the ground I lie. I kiss the earth again. It hath not wounded Me. It takes My tears. It drinks My blood, and doth not cast Me off with scorn. I here lie still and rest My aching heart and agonizing limbs a little ere the traitor comes. I hear his footsteps now. O earth! I lean upon thee. Let Me weep a little more. The fount is open now. My scalding tears will ease the pain that seems like death; and yet I will not, cannot die. O My Judas! O

My people! come not now so fast. Let Me rest a little here till in the earth I dry Mine eyes and gather strength to bear My cross."

O my Jesus! I cannot tell to creatures how these words affrighted me, how they almost took my reason from me. I seemed to lose myself in grief, to be myself an agony. I need not tell to Thee my woe. Thou wilt well remember all. For Thou didst hear my tearful prayer. And when it seemed that life would go where reason fled, and death would come before Thy voice would speak to me again, I heard the tones I love beyond the harps of heaven. They were weaker than before, more full of sadness sweet. I knew they came through tears. Listen, O my trembling heart! my Beloved speaks to me. Let my whole being wait, and kneel before Him with adoring faith! Oh! can I say it, dare I say it now?

I cherish as the dearest gift of God the message that He gave to me. Be still, my every sense! Awake the fires of love. Around the prostrate, bleeding form oh! let them kindle into flame.

My child, these hours of grief are nearly passed. The Olive shades will soon be left alone. I have suffered all. No worse can man inflict. This chalice was not needed to My sacrifice. The souls whom I redeem might spare Me this. They have wounded Me where I am weak. In the tenderest points of that most sacred heart with which I loved them so, they have hurt Me unto death. These wounds will never heal. Oh! they hurt Me so that I can hardly speak. To tell of them is agony, and like the poisoned spear that turns within an open wound. Know you, My child—oh! can you ever know—the awfulness of sin that hurts the heart of God? Know you how your God can feel? I was the victim for their sins. I willed to suffer and to bleed. I was even anxious in My love to die. I spared no sorrow from My life. There was no pain I did not gladly bear. But was it needed they should turn against Me with ingratitude? Could they not have recognized the strength of My affection, and have blessed Me for My blood? And if they could not praise My grace nor thank Me for My cross, was it for them to put to scorn My lowliness, despise My longing love, and trample on My blood as if I were not God, as if I were not even man?

Oh! hast thou ever known the stings that wound so deep within the house of friends? Hast thou, then, tasted that ingratitude which chills the heart and turneth every tenderness to pain? Who are those who wound like friends? A love that could not meet response, despised with rude ingratitude becomes the source of bitterness, and dwells within the wounded heart to be a memory of pain. The hands are open and the breast is bare. The traitor knows where he can strike and leave a wound which time will never heal.

And if thou hast ever known the stings that come from friends, and if thy heart be sore, then think of Me. Compare My love to thine. Compare the little thou hast borne with My great weight of pain. To seek for gratitude, some slight return for all I bore, to look for some affection to console My grief, this was indeed My right. My heart was yearning for some love. Was I not God? Did I not wear the beauty which the angels tremble to adore? Had I not attractions strong enough to win My people to Me? There was never seen on earth a face like Mine. My breast was filled with all the gentleness of God. My words were sweet and tender to bring peace to each afflicted soul. "I did not strive nor cry. I did not break the bruised reed, nor quench the smoking flax." I healed the sick, I raised the dead. I let the mourner lean on Me; and when the light of earth was fled, I turned aside the cloud and showed the broken heart the light of heaven. Why could I fail to win their love? I took their sorrows as Mine own. I died to save them from the wrath of God. I shed My blood to wash them from their stains. I gave them everything I had— My life, My body to be tortured, and My soul to direst agony. My name, My spotless fame, the anguish of My Mother dear, the torments of My saints, were all a sacrifice to cleanse them from their sins and draw them to Mine arms.

O ye benighted race of man! do you not know that God is dying for your sins? And have you known how He can suffer and how He can love?

This is not all the burden of My woe. The death of shame was not enough for Me. This cruel death did not exhaust the yearning of My soul. Before I died My testament was made, and ratified upon the cross. I could not say farewell. I must remain with those so dear to Me, with those My passion bought, with those I washed with blood. My legacy was then indeed Myself. The victim of the cross remains on earth. The sacrifice endures. I give My body and My blood, My soul and My divinity, to be the food of such as will partake of Me. Upon the altars in the rite divine will I be offered to the end of time. Within the tabernacle so lowly and so little shall be seen My home. A prisoner will I dwell with men; and seek for hearts that love, and win them to be Mine. I will change them by My flesh, transform them by My blood. They shall be one with Me, as I am one with God. I can do no more. The Infinite has reached the bounds of power. This is the work of love divine. I do not simply die—I come to live and dwell in them, where My humanity shall be the source of life eternal and of beauty ever new. I clasp them to My breast, and as I embrace their feebleness they change from glory unto glory, when My heart is satisfied and I have taught them how to love.

Now, what return have I for all this wealth of grace, for all this revelation of the yearning of My soul? I have indeed the chalice of ingratitude to drink —ingratitude so deep that God alone can measure it. This was the answer from the race of men, when thus in humbled form, a beggar at their doors, with bleeding hands and feet, I sought their hearts. Oh! this the fearful cup I dreaded so need not have been My agony! I did not ask the Father from My pains to take one pang. I did not seek to put away the spear or nail. I even kissed the cross when ruffian hands were pressing it upon My wounded back. No, I would have suffered more, if that were possible. I only asked for gratitude. Was that too much to ask? Could a sorrowing, dying God, the victim for the sins of men, not ask this boon? My soul cried out in tears: "I ask a little of your love. Is this too much? The Incarnate Word is kneeling to you in His crimson robe? You love the creature god who seeks you for himself; you take the poisoned fruit and flowers that blossom for the grave; you run for honors, and the golden idols which decay; you follow fast the fallen spirits coming from their hell to draw you there. Can you not see your God, revealing you His heart, imploring you to seek the riches that endure, and have your part with angels who are reigning in His light?" From many My response was scorn. They seemed to trample on My blood, and threw their weight on Me, as I lay crushed beneath the wrath that smote Me for their crimes.

I saw the long procession of the lost, the souls I could not save. They stood before Me as I cried for them with sobs and tears. I numbered all their graces costing Me My life, the sins I tried to purge them from, the sorrows that I sought to heal. I followed with a patience which was turned by no ingratitude, with gentleness that might have moved the heart of stone. I gave them sacraments; I threw My blood before them; I even offered them My flesh. It was all in vain. Their lives are now the saddest history of wasted grace. They had love for others, for the things of sense, for the baser pleasures which defile, but none for Me. They accepted every friend, and even leaned on selfish hearts. They rejected Me. They took the creature and refused their God. And now their cup is misery beyond the power of man to know. The flames of hell must burn them to eternity, when one drop of blood I shed had earned them heaven, the joys of bliss with Me. I am wasted on their lost and darkened souls. And in the smoke and fire ascending now before the throne I see their faces full of hate, their hideous writhings with the fangs of demons fierce, or hear the oaths they utter while in their agony they curse My name. O sinners lost! I suffered then for you within the garden and on Calvary! Why could I not have saved you from your awful doom? Why were your hearts so cold to Me, or so unmindful of My grief? Oh! tell Me, what can be the agony of wasted human love? If this be pain, then think of Him who, equal to the Father, and God's only

Son, poured out His blood and broke His heart for you!

The dreadful thought with anguish almost stifles life. It is because I loved them so that they have found the way to hurt Me; that of My heart's great tenderness for them they made the source of all My direst pain. Had I not been their brother in the flesh, how had they pierced Me with the nail and spear? Had I not willed to take the cup of poverty and toil, had they reproached Me for My lowliness? Had I not died that they might live, could they have laughed Me like a criminal to scorn, and even for My cross have learned to treat me with despite? If My precious blood had not been shed like water poured upon the earth, could they have trampled on it, as it begged to heaven for mercy on their souls? Had I not followed them in all their devious ways, seeking them within the desert drear amid the wrecks of crime, could they have turned on Me and called Me beggar, man despised, and not a God? If in their ruin sad I had not held to them the hands divine, when none were near to rescue them; had I not laid them on My bleeding shoulders, aching with the cold, and borne them home without reproach, to cleanse them with My blood, to feed them with My flesh, could they in base ingratitude have spurned My arms, and crimsoned with the current of My life, have run to creature love, and brought defilement where My spotless body once was laid? Had I not sought them starving, freezing with the cold, and taken them to My embrace, and warmed them on My breast, could they have turned to sting and wound Me with the life that came from Me? And in that sacrament divine where I repeat the sorrows of My cross, am daily sacrificed for those I seek to save, how is My wounded heart o'erwhelmed with grief? I am a prisoner at their will. I veil the glories of My deity, and wait on them as if I were the creature bound beneath their bonds, and even less than man. Upon My sacramental throne I reign as if an exile from My Father's court, with few to bow before My lowliness. Alone I wait, forgotten or despised, where angels come to comfort Me, to cheer the sadness of My heart with songs I hear around the throne. Within this prison of My love I sit to see the faithless pass, unmindful of My grief, regardless of My pain. I bear the cross upon My breast; the thorny crown is on My brow; the nails are in My hands and feet; the spear is in My heart. I sit and read the thoughts of men; I taste their base ingratitude. And so Gethsemani comes back to Me, while in My bleeding hands I hold My broken heart. The Olive shades surround Me there while there I dwell to take the chalice which I dreaded so, which in the garden drear convulsed Me with the sweat of blood. Oh! how I suffer now! How deep within My heart this awful sting goes down! Oh! let Me weep awhile. The tears will bring relief. Oh! let Me bow Mine eyes and hide them here. The grass, now reddened with My blood, shall drink the sighs which neither God nor man will hear. It is the hurt which not the hands divine can heal, the fearful wound which, like a flame of fire, is burning in My breast. O My broken, broken heart, so soon to beat no more, I cannot ease thy pain! Take, oh! take thy cup of agony. There is no cure. Thou art wounded unto death.

And then, while tears ran down, the soul seemed parting from the body in a sharper pain than death. I looked to see if there were consolation from the home of friends. And as I looked My hands were pierced anew. I laid them on the chilling grass, as they were burning so. I stretched them out, that I might see the source of this new pain. Alas! I touched the cross, I saw the ruffian with the nails. What home have I on earth? With My Mother was I once for long and blessed years. I was an exile far beyond the sea; but then I laid My wearied head upon her loving breast! Although the Son of God was driven from homes of earth, in poverty ignored, I had a rest within her gentle arms, and it was home to Me to feel her touch and see her smile. Now that home is broken up. She hath no resting-place, and I, her child, must die among the skulls, upon the cross. Her precious hands can never touch Me more till I am dead. She cannot smile on Calvary. No, I have no home on earth. No one so desolate as I. And as I lie upon the ground I feel the footsteps of the traitor as he comes; and, leading on his band with swords and staves, he ventures to betray Me with a kiss. Ah! yes, the faithless soul with smiles will come, and ask from Me the recognition of a friend, the fond embrace with which I used to tell him of My love. This Judas sells Me for a paltry price. I see his heart with avarice possessed. He will deny Me with despair; before My Easter morn shall dawn, the morn that heralds far and wide the everlasting day, he sinks by his own hand among the flames of hell. Oh! can I bear this awful wound, this dire ingratitude! And must I lose on Calvary's height the soul of Mine apostle? Must I be then betrayed by one so near to Me, so dearly loved? O these wounds within My hands! they ache, they smart with anguish dire! Alas! My Judas comes not here alone. There are many traitors in his train. He leads the long procession as they pass with spear and staves. They sell Me to My foes, betray Me for the things of time, prefer the pleasures of the world to Me, and for the honors of the earth deny My faith. They kiss me with their lips, they call themselves My chosen ones, will even boast of that embrace wherewith I bade them rest within My arms, and yet will drive Me from their hearts, and welcome to My throne some sensual god, some spirit lost who only seeks them for the misery of hell.

The more I love the more I feel, and they whom I love most have power to wound Me where the keenest pangs afflict My aching heart. Oh! how I feel the slightest shadow of untruth from them, the slightest coldness to My yearning love. I am all theirs by ties divine; why cannot they be wholly

Mine? Why must I fail to draw them to Myself alone? Am I not God? Can creature love be stronger than the love of God? I must be jealous of the hearts I choose. I cannot see another sit upon My throne. Oh! why, My dearest chosen ones, why wound My soul so sensitive, so full of tenderness? Why must love of self, the vanity of empty pride, sometimes the cravings of the senses, come between Me and your souls? Why am I not alone your end supreme? Why are you so cold to Me, as if My presence were fatigue? Oh! how you hurt Me when I feel that after all My grace, the promises of constancy renewed, the ring you wear in token of a heavenly spouse, the nuptial pledges of our love, I am not the master of your heart. Why must I win you by My tears? Why must I touch you with a bleeding hand and give you pain? Why must I break the idols of the earth and make your home so desolate? Why, oh! why can I not win you by My grace, by the beauty of My face? Why must I weep to look on you? Why choose you not the joyous smile which gladdens heaven? When will you learn what bitter tears you made Me shed. and what it costs to make you true, to hold you as you struggle from My arms? I seek pure souls; and they alone can be the place of My repose. Why must the bitterness of sin bring souls to Me? Why must I ever go to deserts drear to seek My wandering sheep? Why will they renew the sorrows of My path to Calvary? Why must I bear them on My bleeding shoulders as My cross, and tremble with their coldness, as My hands and feet are aching with their wounds? Oh! how it costs Me pain to purify their souls from stain, and lead them, as I must, through paths of penitence, to make them feel a little of My grief and bear a portion of the cross with Me! Some souls are true and willing in this tearful way! My wounded heart will tell to God; it cannot tell to thee, the love I have for virgin hearts who are indeed My brides, who have no love but Mine—My saints who walk beside Me, looking always on My face. I clasp their hands in Mine. I am with them in shadows dark, in winter's cold, in summer's heat, in all the struggles of their life, in all the agonies of death. And when I look beyond the grave, and see the sinless fire My hands have kindled for Mine own, see how My chosen suffer there, oh! think you not that I am hurt indeed? They suffer so for their ingratitude, because they were not faithful to My grace, because at times they chose another love than Mine. These spots upon their raiment white are marks of infidelity to Me. My flowing tears could not wash out the stain. My tender heart was not enough. The powers of sense were stronger than their vows to God. There must be fire whose searching strength shall burn the dross and leave the gold in virgin purity. And yet these agonizing fires need not have been for them! They might have given Me their hearts and never hurt Me with the stings of coldness or ingratitude.

Upon My sacramental throne I sit by day and night, the God of love, the prisoner bound in hand and foot. I yearn to give My light and heat, to cheer the darkened soul with rays from heaven, to speak as God made man alone can speak to every suffering heart. Oh! how My wounded breast is bleeding there, while I thus sit alone, with none but angels to adore, or kneel to pray My erring children home, or stand to bless the pilgrim as he presses on to Me! In that divine repose, where I am all for those I love, the fountain flowing full cf pity infinite, the source of strength where flesh is weak, I waste the tenderness which springs at every moment new. The treasure of My heart is neither felt nor known. Sometimes I am ignored, sometimes forgotten. It wearies so the flesh to spend one hour with Me. My children dear, they call Me Spouse; they speak of My affection as their right; they say there is no love like Mine, and yet they cannot come and kneel before Me as the lover to the loved; they cannot bid the earth retire, and think of Me alone! I see them wearied as they kneel. The garden scene is ever wounding Me, where I am weakest in My love. They are sleeping like the three apostles when the shadows fell. With heavy eyes they are unconscious of My grief for them. And when they come to take Me as their food, and My whole being springs with joy to give them all I have and am, how coldly do they come! How chilling to My warm affection their response! What have they to say to Me when in all the ardor of a love divine I speak to them, when My hands are eager to embrace them in a fond caress and pour My wealth upon their souls? Are they indeed like lovers to their heavenly Spouse? Sometimes I hear no words, sometimes I see no tears, sometimes their thoughts are wandering far from Me; they seem unmindful that the Bridegroom comes, that God is loving them as He alone can love. O My heart! the heart of God, how dost thou waste thy grace! The wealth of deity, the riches that make glad the courts of heaven, are thus unknown, unseen of men on earth.

And now, my child, I will not tell thee of thyself. The lesson thou hast learned within these awful shades, where thou hast seen a little of My bitter pain, will teach thee of thy share within the wounded heart of thy Beloved. I grieve and yet I love to see thee weep, as here thou dost recall the many stings thy faithlessness has sharpened for My breast. Thou wilt remember all thy wandering steps, the idols thou hast worshipped in My stead, the creatures that as shadows came to dim My light, the hours when I was not thy Love supreme. Thy sobs are hurting Me as here I lie so weak; and yet thy tears are washing out the marks of guilt. The shadows are departing one by one. The idols are in ruins here. The wrecks of thine inconstancy are in this garden strewn. Thou wilt not touch again the snares thou hast forsaken here. The creature love is dead for ever now. It shall not arise again. Thou shalt go with Me to Calvary. Thou shalt see Me die. The nails that hold Me to the cross shall fasten thee to Me. Thou shalt wound My heart no more.

Now, my new-born child thus bathed in blood, I here accept thy vows. Kneel here in truth. Reach out thy hand to Me. Thou canst not see Me as I touch thee in this night of pain. Yet thou canst hear and feel. Hold fast to Me! I come to put My ring upon thy hand. Does the pledge of Mine espousals pain? The finger bleeds which I shall press. Look well and see—not thy blood is flowing here, but Mine! Oh! strange indeed this bridal chamber of thy King, the garden of His woe, the deepest shadows of Gethsemani! The music of the nuptial song the sobs of thy Beloved! The marriage-garment crimsoned with His blood! The words of His espousals the sad language of a wounded heart! And now I have a moment only to prepare. Kneel here, My loving child, beside Me. I can speak no more. It eases the sharp pain consuming Me to know that thou art here. Oh! dost thou truly love Me now? Then let Me hold thy hand one moment more. Alas! the traitor's steps I hear. My face is swollen and My lips are red. I must kiss him when he comes. One moment more, My precious child, to tell Me of your love while I bow down My aching head and hold My breaking heart. One more sob, and life would go before the time. My Father, come to Me and I will weep no more! The chalice of My agony I give back to Thee. Behold Thy Son has drunk its dregs. Oh! chase away the clouds, and let Mine angels come.

My cup of fear, of loneliness, of sadness drear, of awful pain, the stings that pierce the heart divine—I offer all to Thee for those I love. Let them draw near in this My nuptial hall, amid the drooping olive-trees. Then touch, oh! for an instant touch the harps of heaven, and let Me hear the songs that cheer the Bridegroom's breaking heart. And then, as all is ready, let the wondrous rite proceed.

Bow down, O ye bright angels of My court! and to this garden come. This is indeed the garden of My loves; and here in fertile soil the flowers shall bloom to smile upon the banks of crystal streams where I shall lead My virgin train, the spouses of My agonizing soul. For a moment let the shadows of My cross depart; let the rays of heavenly light descend; let the Seraphim and Cherubim in bright array begin their song. It is the Word of God, the Word made flesh, that bleeds and dies upon His wedding-day.

Meditation Seventh.

JESUS CONDEMNED TO DEATH.

MEDITATION SEVENTH.

JESUS CONDEMNED TO DEATH.

"He was offered because it was His own will: He shall be led as a sheep to the slaughter, and shall be dumb as a lamb before his shearer, and He shall not open His mouth."— ISAIAS liii. 7.

My heart was filled with peace and joy unlike the sweetness I had sometimes known before. Oh! was it joy amid the scenes of this Gethsemani? I know not what it was. My Blessed Master seemed so near to me; and when He told me of the nuptial rite, I felt the pressure of His hands, and I seemed borne away, away from all things sensible. Did the bliss of heaven come then an instant to expel the sadness from my soul? I cannot tell. My lips were moving to one word, "Jesus, Master, my

Beloved, draw me close to Thee. Am I going to the altar now with Thee? Are these the wedding garments for my King? Shall I behold Him in His beauty here? Jesus, Master, how I love Thee now!" I dare not speak of what He seemed to say to me. How could He embrace me so, and to one like me pour out the sweetness which entranced my soul, my will, my every faculty? If this be not the paradise I seek, oh! what shall be the joy when earth and sorrow shall be past, and I shall see my Jesus as He is? O love divine! Thou art indeed the Word made Flesh. Thou art my Spouse, my Master, and my God. I feel the breath of angels near, while their celestial arms are holding me that I may live. I am so blest, and yet I do not die.

I was looking up to heaven with straining eyes. It seemed there was no earth. Some strong attraction fixed my gaze, and for the fulness of my sight I could not see. Then suddenly, I know not when, I know not how, the vision ceased and I awoke. I was in the garden still, and yet the blessed place was not so dark. The rays that had entranced me so were not all gone. I was kneeling still where I had knelt so long. I was confused in mind. My memory seemed gone. I tried to gather up the broken threads and to recall what I had seen. This is the garden still. It is not gone. Here is the place of prayer. Think, my soul, you have not moved. Here was your Beloved laid. Here you saw His sweat of blood. Here He told you of His agony. Mark well the olive-trees. Can they ever be forgotten? Yes, I said, it is the place. It is Gethsemani. I am not moving now, yet I am coming back. Oh! yes, I see, and yet the cloud is gone! My sight begins to grow upon me. I can hear a little, too. What are the sounds that fall upon my senses now? There are voices sweet and sad, unlike the tones of earth. If I do not hear, I feel the harmony of some celestial song. Oh! thanks to God, I see some angel forms. They fill me with their peace. They are kneeling now. I cannot see my Master dear as they surround Him, bowing to the earth with adoration. And I am kneeling, too, with them. O my Beloved! let them tell with their angelic tongues how I adore Thee, how my life with all its powers goes up to Thee. They are speaking now. I could not hear their words. Was it praise or prayer? I cannot tell. It was the angels' offering to their King laid low. I tried to join my feeble voice when thus I felt the melody of heaven that floated in the air around my Master sad and bleeding from a wounded heart. And then I watched and prayed. O Thou my sorrowing Love! wilt thou arise? I heard Thee speak of Calvary, the weary road that lay before Thee. How long upon the ground shall my Redeemer lie, as if it were His bed of death? I saw the angels bow their heads and kiss the earth, and then He rose in majesty divine. O my Jesus! let me look at Thee. Oh! give me strength to see Thee as Thou art. These eyes are Thine, always and for ever Thine.

He gave me strength. I saw His face once more. He turned and looked at me and smiled. Oh! could I paint Him as He stood, so meek and pale, and stained with blood! His face was sad, and yet it wore the majesty of God. His form was bent, His limbs moved feebly as with pain; His hands were folded on His breast, His finger pointed to His heart. I yearned to run and throw my adoration at His feet. I could not move! The angels held me back.

The hour to kneel with spirits blest had not yet come. He takes His hands from their repose upon His breast; He lifts them once again. The angels kneel. They kiss the ground once more. No word they speak. The light celestial is departing. I feel their pinions moving on the air; and they are gone.

I looked again. The darkness had returned. I could see no more, and yet I felt my Blessed Jesus there. I knew He stood alone. My dearest Love, I cried, what can I do? I will never leave Thee; Thou wilt never cast me off. Where Thou goest I will go, and if Thou shalt here abide I will remain with Thee. Oh! let me be as angels at Thy side to comfort Thee. Listen to my plaint of love. I come, my Jesus, I will come, and where the seraphim were kneeling I will bow my head.

He looked at me as He had never looked before. He drew me with that sad face, and yet He held me back. He looked beyond me through the garden. My precious child, He said, you do not see nor hear. I have taken up your senses all, and hid them in My breast. Look there beyond you. See the torches gleam. Hear the tread of armed men. Their shouts are breaking on the air that now was filled with angels' song. They are pressing through these sacred shades. They will seize Me, bind Me with their ropes, beat Me with their staves, and drag Me off to death. Farewell, My child. My hour is come; remember what I am to thee; be brave and follow Me to Calvary.

I turned away, but not away from Him. I was frightened at the noise I heard. Who could be profane enough to come with spear and sword within these sacred shades, where He had suffered so, where His precious blood had reddened all the earth, where the grass had taken up His tears, where He was exhausted unto death? Yes, who leads this ruffian band, with faces coarse, with language vile? Alas! the traitor comes before them. It is Judas, the apostle; well he knows this garden of His Master's woe. With rapid tread and fearful face, as if some spirit lost possessed him, he is hurrying on. The lanterns shine like eyes of evil fire. O Judas! stay thy course! It is not too late! The spear of your ingratitude has surely pierced His breast. Go kneel as you have often knelt before. Ask pardon for your foul offence, and you may feel the grace with which this garden fills the earth. Stay, thou traitor to thy God; He will reveal His person here, and in the majesty divine will stand before thee! Then I saw my mighty King as He arose, and raised His arm to heaven, and looked upon His enemies. The torches fell, the spears and clubs were strewn upon the ground, and Judas and his band were as the dead. For a moment Jesus paused and held His arm above them as the glory of the Highest passed before me. My soul was full of praise. Triumphant songs were on my lips. "O my Beloved Lord!" I cried, "Thou art the King! Let these foes of Thine lie dead before Thee. Let not the ruffians touch Thy sacred flesh. Send them far away to darkness drear where spirits of the night shall bind them hand and foot. Let even Judas fall! What flame of hell is fierce enough to burn his treason out? Oh! I cannot let the traitor touch Thee, tender Master and my Friend. Give me the spear and let me stand in deadly strife before him here!" It was but an instant that I waited then My Jesus held me still. The air of majesty supreme was gone, and on His gentle face the look of sad submission reigned. I heard Him say: "Whom seek ye, friends? I am Jesus; it is My dearest name. Take Me at your will, and let My children leave in peace." Then my Blessed Master stood alone. The disciples were awake from sleep. The sound of arms had roused them in dismay. Some passed on and hid themselves amid the trees. James and John were valiant to the last, and came behind their Lord, while Peter drew the sword and struck for life. With kindling eyes the Master saw the wound that Peter made. He touched the bleeding gash and healed the foe, and sheathed the sword. "Not now to fight for Me. The Lamb of God is offered by His will. The martyr's crown shall wait for you when He is gone. They cannot touch Me here unless I will. I have shown them now that I am God. Then let Me yield Myself, and, as the sheep to slaughter led, the Eternal Son shall in their hands be dumb."

Oh! then I saw the sight which like a fire is burning in my brain. I saw the treason reach its highest crime. I saw the kiss of love become the sign of foulest treachery. Oh! can I ever blot from memory's page this awful scene? My blessed Jesus stood so meek before the clamorous band. With eyes cast down, with sadness inexpressible, with sweetness all divine, He crossed His arms upon His breast and waited for the traitor. I saw Judas go to meet Him. What will he do? Will he dare to touch my Lord? Ah! he will do more. I heard him say, turning to the leaders of his band: "Whomsoever I shall kiss, that same is He. Then forward come, and bind Him fast." Oh! I cried, it must not, cannot be! He shall not kiss the dearest lips on earth and heaven, the swollen, bleeding lips of

my Beloved. I cannot bear it! The
sight will kill me! I will run now and
hold him fast. My trembling arms shall
be as bands of iron to prevent this
sacrilege. O my precious Love! I will
go before his stealthy steps; he shall
not touch the lips that are the joy of
angels! I tried to move. I could not
stir. Some power invisible restrained
my feet while in my grief I saw this
outrage on my Lord. O Judas! fear:
the day of deep remorse shall come.
The worm that never dies shall sting
thee with its cruel fangs. Alas! I saw
the traitor meet the look of pity from My
Jesus' face with eyes of stone. I heard
him say: "O Rabbi, hail!" I saw his
lips upon the mouth of my most precious Love. "Oh!" in ardent grief I cried
—"oh! shall this traitor vile, who loves
Thee not, presume to take the kiss for
which the saints and angels sigh? Oh!
that I could pass between this Judas and

my Lord; that I might kiss the blessed lips with all the love my soul could utter to Thee! Then could I die in bliss. I cannot bear to see the vile approach Thee. Thou art the Prince of hearts, the everlasting King! And I will weep mine eyes away that I am bound and cannot here avenge this outrage on my Lord." Then did Jesus meekly speak to Judas, called him friend, and one more warning gave: "O Mine apostle! has it come to this? Is this the mark of Mine affection turned to treachery base? With the kiss of love dost thou betray Me here, and is there no remembrance of the past to lead thee to repentance? O Judas! wait. The Victim of the cross is near. The tree of life is planted here, and near its root the flames of hell are burning for thee. Must I lose thee, then, for ever?"

Then He turned to me, and, while the tenderness of love was sounding in

His voice, there was the shadow of reproach. "My child, thou didst promise to be brave, to follow Me where I should lead. Go not, then, before Me, nor anticipate My ways. Thou hast much to see and much to hear. If this outrage to My lips so saddens thee, what wilt thou do when thou shalt see Me beaten, mocked, mutilated with the cruel scourge, fainting, dying on the cross? You must follow Me and pray for courage and for grace. You may love Me with a weeping heart; but the Master leads; and where the Lamb is dumb the child must never speak. Look at my sorrowing face with tears; watch My bending form as long as sight shall last. I will know that you are near, and I will see your looks of love. My fainting heart shall to the last accept the incense which ascends from yours. But stir not a hand or foot to take Me from My foes, nor come between the spears now levelled at My breast. Follow Me, as dumb as I, and I will show thee how thy God can die."

I did not move. I had no power. I saw the traitor point at my Beloved. I saw the ruffians seize Him with a rudeness vile, as if some beast of prey were in his rage. My Master gave them such a look of pity and of pain, as He held out His arms that they might bind them fast, and bowed His glorious head that they might take Him at their will. Oh! those blessed arms, so dear to me—the arms that had embraced me in my grief—they were pinioned now! And He, so weak, fainting with the loss of blood, exhausted with His agony, is bound indeed. Great ropes are tied around His waist. They tear Him with their cruel tension. He can scarcely breathe. Then I hear a laughter and the shout of scorn, as they drag Him with the ropes away. "The Nazarene is ours," they cry. "He can no more escape. We will hurry Him to prison and to death." I watched my blessed Master as they forced Him on. He turned and looked upon the Olive shades once more, as if to say farewell. I thought He looked at me, and as my tears flowed on I could not then restrain my heart. I was forced to kneel where He had knelt before I followed in His steps. I could not leave this sacred watch of prayer, the place of my espousals to my Love, until I kissed the earth which He had touched, until my aching head was bowed where He had lain, until my streaming eyes should feel the tears which He had shed. Oh! it is too much for one like me to be where Thou hast been. Dearest Lord, I must stay here. How can I go away? This garden is my home. I cannot bear the light of earth again. And then my senses seemed to fail. I fell unconscious on the ground, and as I touched the crimsoned turf my sight was gone. There came an awful faintness, as my trembling lips could form no word. I seemed going, going far from all things seen. I was running in a fearful haste to catch my Master's sorrowing face, which passed before me like the light.

O my Jesus dear! Thou art gone, but I will overtake Thee. My rapid breathing now is agony; I will not lose Thee. I will die without Thee here! And then I heard the shouts again, the sound of armed men, the curses rising on the air. Where was I now? I was running fast, and breathless with fatigue. The torches gleamed before me, and the crowd was pushing on. I turned and tried to see my way. The garden was no more. How came I here so far from Him? The brook is passed, and here the city's walls stand frowning at me.

Where am I going, then, and where, oh! where is my Beloved? He could not think me traitor, that I was not brave enough to follow Him, that I did not love Him well enough to stay until the end! How long was I unconscious then? I ran with eager haste; I followed as the crowd surrounded me, and soon I found myself before the court of Annas. How I entered there, or how the rabble gave me place, I could not tell. My heart was leading me to my Beloved. And when I saw Him there, His hands so rudely bound, His head bowed down, His face so meek, I yearned to throw myself before His feet, that I might share His mockery; for they were mocking Him with jeer and oath profane. They called Him traitor to the Jews, the prophet false, the leader of sedition. He answered not a word. The Lamb of God indeed was dumb. I could not see His blessed face, His head was so bent down; His eyes seemed closed. To the laughter, to the curse, no answer came. I tried to speak for Him. The words rushed even to my lips: "Jesus, Master, let me plead for Thee." The power of speech was gone; the thought of words alone remained. Suddenly I heard a loud and furious cry. "Bind Him fast and drag Him out!" I heard them shout. The ropes were tightened in their cruel haste. I saw Him pant for breath. I knew that He could scarcely stand. I heard Him fall, and then I saw them beat Him with their staves, and pull Him up, and rudely drag Him on. Oh! what evil hath He done? Where, ye ruffians vile, where will ye drag Him now? I know not how I lived. It was not I! Some power unseen was moving me, as like one dead I travelled on. I seemed to see His sad and tearful face, and yet I did not see. I seemed to touch the ropes that dragged Him on, as if I were bound. And yet there were no ropes around my hands or feet. And yet I was not free. O blessed bonds! if I am bound with Thee, Thou Lover of my soul! I care not where they force my steps, if I may go with Thee! I could not tell the way. My mind has failed. Was I in prayer for my Beloved, or had I lost the faculty of thought? What is this wondrous scene before me now? It is a palace vast. There are the seats of judgment all arranged; the great high-priest is sitting here, and all the glory of the Aaronic line appears in state. My heart is sinking at the sight, as I behold my Master standing there alone. No friend is near. He is looking down. He will not raise His eyes. He will not speak. There is the clamor of an angry crowd. I could not hear their words. I saw the form of Caiaphas as he arose and seemed to question Him. Is this the last of that grand priestly line? thought I. The glories of the Aaronic ministry, are they to end in this sad scene? Oh! how I yearned to stand beside my Master then, to be His advocate and plead for Him! O ye benighted priests! do ye not know that He who is arraigned before you is the Son of God, the Virgin's Child of prophecy, the Christ so long foretold? And then I thought I saw the olden times, the blazing mountain in the wilderness, the tabernacle filled with heavenly light, the temple with its glories from on high, the golden mercy-seat where dwelt the cloud of fire. And as I looked, before me passed the long procession of the Levite race, and Aaron, robed in sacerdotal vestments, led the train. "Farewell to all the mighty past," he cried. "This is our dying day. Before us stands the Eternal Priest; the types shall vanish in His light.

Yet oh! the curse that falls upon our race when consecrated hands shall bind the Lord of all, when consecrated lips shall sentence Him to death." And as before mine eyes this vision passed, I seemed to see the finger of the great high-priest, as, pointing to the form of my Beloved, he was gone. There came a mournful chant upon my ears: "This is the end. The top of Sinai bathed in light, the mountain flaming with the lightning's flash, is here transformed. The lamb no more shall bleed upon the mercy-seat; the veil that hides the face of God is rent in twain. The Lamb of God is here, condemned to die; with Calvary's fearful crime the glories of our priesthood end in blood." The vision passed; I looked upon my Master, as He stood accused, without a word in His defence. It was the last great council of the Jewish state, and Caiaphas arose to speak the words of doom. In all the grandeur of his sacerdotal robes he bade the clamorous crowd be still: "No more of laugh and jeer. What say you of the Nazarene? Think you that He is dumb, or that in pride He will not answer make to God's highpriest? I will adjure Him by the living God! Art Thou the Christ by prophecy foretold, the great Jehovah's blessed Son?" Then, indeed, I saw the majesty divine like flame of fire enkindling in the face of my Beloved. His precious features gleaming as the sun at noon, He raised His head in all the dignity of deity; His form was lifted up as if He stood upon a cloud whose golden hue encompassed Him like glittering curtains of the morn. I trembled as I saw His so transfigured face, and all my love in highest adoration bowed before Him. Oh! the Lamb is dumb no more. The Eternal Priest will speak.

The dying line of Aaron's race shall hear: "I am the Son of God. I am the Christ foretold, the Virgin's Child and Israel's King. Your fathers have expected Me. I am the Paschal Lamb. The priesthood now to cease in woe beneath the wrath of Heaven has told of Me in every sacred rite, in every victim's blood, in every sacrificial prayer. The altar speaks of Me; the temple's majesty is but the type of My humanity. I am your David's root; I am the bright and morning star. Before the patriarchal day I am. I am the victim now. The Lamb of God is led to slaughter by His own will. Fulfil your doom. Condemn your God to death. Behold Me standing here upon the cloud. My hands are bound, My feet are tied. There are none to plead My cause. Look well upon the Nazarene, your King. The great Jehovah of your fathers stands before your bar.

The hour shall come. The cloud that gathers as a throne beneath His mangled feet shall rise, and span the heavens with flame. The dead, awaking from their graves, shall march in fear before His seat. The earth itself shall quake, the rocks of ages melt, the elements consume in fire. The armies of the Lord in burning ranks shall kneel before His feet. The voice of the Eternal Father shall proclaim Him King. The Lamb so lowly now shall bid the song begin: "Lift up, ye everlasting gates! The Prince of glory comes. Behold Him sitting on the throne. Adore His face, ye Cherubim and Seraphim. Welcome to the seat of power; welcome to His endless reign."

O my Jesus! how I blessed Thee for this word, for the glory that encompassed Thee in this sad hour. I thought I felt the angels come and kneel before Thee. Mine eyes were

with the vision blest. I seemed to see
the saints of ancient days, prophets,
priests, and kings, as in this judgment-
hall they crowded round Thee. My
heart was full of love and pride. My
Master dear, my God, my King, was
taking to Himself the robes of glory.
Was the Prisoner divine indeed set
free? Oh! let me see! Where has my
vision gone? Does He ascend from
sorrow now? Are the heavens parting
to receive Him with His train? Shall I
be with my Love when the golden
doors shall open to the music of His
voice? Oh! I will see. I will mark
Him well. The cruel ropes, are they
upon Him still?

I strained my eyes. A cloud had
blinded me. I could only hear. What
tones are these that come to vibrate on
the void which He had filled? It
sounds like herald's cry in notes of
doom. It was the great high-priest

who spoke, the council in its state around Him. So awful were the words I seemed to hear, that reason trembled fearfully as if possessed of horrid dreams, or by the spectres of the night bewildered. They called my God blasphemer, and on every side arose the angry shout, "He shall die; the Nazarene shall die!" Surely these are not the tones of men alone, not the sentence of the priests. I hear the unearthly howl of demons, as amid an awful chorus the refrain comes back: "The Nazarene blasphemes! He shall die! He shall die!"

Where was my blessed Master now while thus the jeers of earth and hell surrounded Him? At first I could not see; and then when prayer was strong, and love like fire was burning up my heart, the vision came. He was bending down beneath their blows. Like ravenous beasts they rushed, they caught Him by the ropes that held Him, dragged Him down and fell upon Him. I heard the sound that rent my heart as with their hands they beat His precious face. The priests went out and left Him to the fury of the ruffian crowd. It was now the noon of night, and so they mocked Him till the dawn. I heard their voices coarse call Him blasphemer. I heard the laugh when in derision loud they called Him prophet and saluted Him as King. I saw them one by one with language vile draw near and spit upon Him! Where was I then to see a sight like this and live? That precious face so dear to me, the sunlight of my soul, was with their spittle, mixed with mire, defiled. His cheeks were swollen with the bruise; His eyes were nearly closed. He could not raise His hands to wipe away the tears, to stanch the blood, for they were bound.

O my dearest Love! I prayed, let me draw near with all the tenderness which I have learned from Thee! I love Thy face above the power of words to tell. Can I see it thus disfigured with the scorn of men? Oh! I am now like Thee: I am dumb; I cannot speak; but let me come, and Thy poor weeping child will bless Thee in eternity. Oh! if I could dare to kiss away the spittle and the mire! Oh! give me, Lord, the treasure of one tear! They must not touch the face divine; they shall not mock my God. O my Master! give me strength, and I will come.

His arms, so firmly bound, were strong enough to hold me back. He did not open once His mouth. There was not a word to hear, but blows were falling fast, and falling on my heart as they smote Him.

There was a voice within my soul that ruled my every sense. My Love divine needs not the use of words. "My precious child," He said, "beware! This is the demons' hour. I am their sport. They are mocking Me because I bear the sinner's part. You see they hurt Me with their staves, tear Me with their thongs, bruise Me with their hands. I feel as God alone can feel the outrage to My face. Their spittle rests within Mine eyes, runs down upon My mouth. Who now would recognize this face of Mary's Child? My tears are freely shed. I cannot keep them back, for oh! My agonizing heart is taking up a sorrow new. There is a pang that stings Me now and quite o'erwhelms Me. I must bid the angels come unseen to hold Me up a little, lest I fall. Think you it is this mockery which thus unnerves My strength, this scorn which opens up the fountain of My tears? Oh! no. I bear full well these jeers that come from foes. The wounds within My hands, they ache the most. My friend, My great apostle, leader of My little band, hath thrice denied Me, hath denied Me with an oath. I heard that oath above the curses of this angry crowd, and it hath struck My heart. I can hear no other sound. The awful words are ringing in My ears. I cannot shut them out: 'I know Him not; I am not His; I have never been with Him; I know Him not.'

"I saw how demons dire surrounded him in conflict fearful to his soul. He could have died for Me; but when I sheathed his sword and tried his tender heart, the light of hope gave out and courage failed. He is repenting now; but yet the words are spoken. His Master, bound, despised, and mocked, arraigned before the council of the state, condemned to death, he hath denied. Oh! the agony of this sad fall; it hurts My love, it makes My heart to bleed. Its bitterness is crushing him. Remorse like angry clouds is shutting out the rays of heaven. The hosts of hell are bidding him despair. I will help him with My pity sweet. I am sending graces strong to hold him up. The flood of light from out My sorrowing soul is drawing near to cheer his penitence. I will take the gloom and send him peace. Go, angels bright who wait My will, on whom I lean amid these awful mockeries — go bind his wounds, go lead him here. Let Me look with My divine affection; let Me heal the sorrow which My tears alone can cure. I will show to him My face. The lines of grief are there. They cannot fade away so soon. But in My weeping eyes he shall behold a pardon full, a mighty love he never saw before.

He shall see how I forgive; I take him closer to My breast, and for his fearful fall he shall the stronger, dearer be. Look! there he comes. See how changed he is. He hath grown old within one night. He walks with trembling steps, as if he feared to come. He little knows My angels hold him up. His form is bent. He cannot raise his head. His tears like torrents flow. He cannot speak. How could he speak above the din of jeer, and oath, and blows? His heart is full of prayer, and I, his God, can hear! See, he tries to kneel; the angels raise him up. Slowly, fearfully his head is turned to Me. I am thus helping him to lift his swollen eyes and look on Me. See now the anguish of that face, the deep remorse, the promise of fidelity, of constancy to death."

My Master looked on him! O sweetest spirits of the heavenly court! let your sympathy divine surround my blessed Love, to praise Him where I fail, for such a look as that! Beneath the blows He stood, the mire and spittle on His face, with form so crushed, as if His heart was welling tears. There came a look so full of tenderness, that depths of mercy infinite revealed the majesty of God; that gentleness like gems of uncreated light was sitting on His royal brow; and on His precious mouth there spoke the pity of a soul divine. Who could withstand that look? O my Jesus dear! how can I thank Thee that I saw Thee then? I had often watched Thy blessed face. I have followed Thee in sorrows drear. I have seen Thee in Thy woes; and every time I looked on Thee the mighty power of Thine attractions hath revealed some treasure new of Thine untold grace. I had often prayed that I might only look, and never even speak. How can I speak when I am lifting up my eyes to Thee? Yet now I see upon Thy bruised and mangled face, so sad and yet so full of sweet compassion, the pardon God alone can give. O gentle Shepherd! how I love Thee now! Thou dost find a joy to seek Thy wandering flock. Thou dost not mind the aching of Thy wounds, the bleeding of Thy hands and feet and shoulders bare. Thou art leading home the pastor of the sheep. That strong and earnest soul shall faint no more. Let one like me, the price of Thine indulgent love, kneel here and pray and weep. Oh! well I know that tender look was not alone for Thine apostle in his fall. It was for me! He did deny Thee once. I have denied Thee many times. In the face of danger, when all earth and heaven arrayed themselves against his Lord, his courage failed. I, poor wayward child, have turned from Thee for things of sense. No foe was near. No danger frightened me. I did forget that Thou wast mine, and in deed, if not in word, I said, "I know Thee not." With those who crucified my God I walked. Sometimes there was a god of gold, sometimes a sensual god; sometimes I bowed my heart, espoused to Thee, to pride. Sometimes Thy tender hands were holding me, and I have wrestled with Thy grace that I might break away from Thee and Thy restraints. Now, in bitterness of deep remorse, I kneel before Thee, O my Master dear! I never knew till now the depth of my inconstancy. With Thine apostle, so convulsed with grief, let me bow down. I have seen Thy pardoning face. It hath moved me, too. Thou hast touched the spring that in the time to come shall never cease to flow. The fountain of repenting tears is open now. Oh! let me hide myself awhile. I cannot leave Thee here, but I will hide from all but Thee. Oh! that the clouds that cover Thee could fall upon me now, and like a mantle drear conceal my weeping eyes from all but Thine! With all my heart I bless Thee for this look! The pastor of Thy flock, the vicar of Thy grace, shall be my guide. His tears shall intercede for mine.

My Master heard my prayer. There came a cloud indeed and hid me in its folds. It was not the blackness of the sky. It was not the absence of the light. It was not a simple solitude where all created things had ceased to be. The waters of remorse engulfed my soul. I saw my sins as one by one they crushed me with their fearful weight. Each infidelity of all my life; each act or word wherein I had denied the heavenly Bridegroom dear to whom

I plighted all my heart; each coldness to His yearning grace, all came before me now. I saw them in my Master's face. I read them in His tears. They then awoke to voice and spoke to me in sighs, the sobs of my afflicted Lord. Deeper, deeper grew the gloom. Down, down the opening chasm did I fall. And yet the light of hope was burning in my soul; for, as senses failed and sight was gone, I saw that look of mercy sad, of that compassion infinite.

How long this cloud was covering me I cannot tell. It seemed an age, as if the countless years had travelled on their march while I lay weeping, hidden in the depths, conscious only of my sin and my unworthiness of Him. When I awoke the night had passed. Where am I now? I cried. Is this the light of day? I thought that day had ceased to be. Oh! tell me, is it day? And if this be day, how is it measured by the stars! Oh! did the sun arise? I thought the sun had died. And if this be light, oh! tell me where I am; where is my Master now? Stop! I do begin to see! Hark! I seem to hear. Oh! am I coming back to life? Then tell me what is life?

What sounds are these I hear? What are these palace walls? Surely this is not the council-chamber of the Jews! I cannot bring to life my senses dim. These halls are strange to me. How came I here? I did not know that I had moved. And now again upon my ears resounds the clamor of a crowd. I feel my Blessed Lord is here. Hark! I hear His precious name. And voices coarse accusing Him of blasphemy demand His death. An awful shout with angry oaths comes up like frantic rage of demons in the flames of hell: "Let Him be crucified! Away with David's

Son! Let Jesus die, like one accursed, upon the cross!"

This fearful cry awoke my wondering mind. My sight returned. Surely these are Roman soldiers standing on their guard. I see the conquering eagle gleam above their ranks. They form in close array around a throne where sits in solemn pomp the representative of Cæsar's power. The captive race, the pride of God's elect, bows down to pagan sway. Jerusalem, in bondage vile, demands the crucifixion of its King. How came I here in Pilate's court? How was my Beloved dragged from cruel mockery, from blows and scorn, to this dread scene? Oh! is His death so near? He told me of His cross, and yet my sluggish, loving heart could never follow Him. Alas! the end is nigh. I must see Him once again. O angels! lift me up above the crowd, above this failing sight, that yet again my eyes may rest on Him, my Master and my God, my only Love! I know not how it was. I am as blind as those that never saw. I am as dumb as those that never spoke. The darkness passed. There came a ray of light, and in its beams I saw the form majestic of my Lord. I saw again His blessed face. He stood in bonds before the judgment throne. The Judge of quick and dead is on His trial now. His eyes were looking up as if to scenes beyond the earth. There was a sadness dark as night upon His brow, while peace that seemed the eternal calm of God was reigning there. O Master dear! indeed I kneel before you now. Your loving child is at your feet. He cannot speak. He scarcely lives. He is all for Thee. What happened then I do not know. I thought I kissed His precious feet, until the tears had told

Him of my new-born love. How can this happiness be mine? I cried. I here have found my home. Nor earth nor heaven can tear me from my Master's feet. I was so happy then, although my heart was panting with its grief. Precious, precious feet, my hands shall hold you fast for ever!

Suddenly I heard another voice, when Pilate rose. "Ye stubborn race of Jews, why seek you this man's life? I see no cause of death. I hear your angry cries. Your witnesses are false. You free the murderer vile. You ask the pardon of the lowest criminal on this your festal day. Like raging beasts you cry against the Nazarene. You are thirsting for His blood. You shall satiate your thirst. Here, guards, go take Him to the pillar in the court. There bind Him fast. Let Him be scourged. Mind not the Roman law; He is a Jew. He seems scarcely living now. If He survive this loss of blood, this deathlike pain, you cannot ask that He be crucified."

These awful words aroused me from my dear repose. I seemed to hold His precious feet, now moistened by my tears ; and when I touched them with my lips some mighty strength renewed the courage of my love. The words of Pilate were a knell to me. I struggled hard to hold the feet that now were dearer to my heart than life itself. I was foolish then. I little knew how weak I was. Oh! cried I, take *me!* Take me in my Master's place. I will bleed or die for Him ; let me be scourged. My precious Jesus, may Thy loving child do this for Thee?

I heard no word as from the blessed feet I sought His face. There was a look that spoke a full response. It was not reproach. It was not surprise. It seemed to say: "You know not what you ask. You could not bear one blow, unless the scourge should first fall heavily on Me. Did I bring you once from deserts wild, a wandering sheep? Where is the pasture of My flock, the home within My heart, unless these shoulders bleed? How often have the senses led you into sin, and vanities of earth beguiled you from My arms! These sins are laid upon my shoulders bare. The scourge alone can draw the blood that washes them away. Oh! let Me go, My child; you cannot hold Me now. Unloose My feet. I go to be baptized indeed for you."

The ruffians rushed like maddened beasts of prey. They tore me from my Lord. With cruel violence they dragged Him out. Within the hall and in the courts their shout resounds: "Unto the scourge, the Nazarene! Yet slay Him not. Go tear Him with the thongs and let Him freely bleed, but spare Him for the cross. With criminals among the skulls, there let Him die!"

The scene that passed before me then no tongue of mine can tell. I know not how I lived, and yet I did not live. I thought I died, and yet it was not death. There was no judgment scene. The face of the celestial King was hid. There were no angels there. I did not even feel the spirits of the air. I can only try to speak, and yet the words are strange to me, as if some other lips than mine were speaking them. Oh! give me aid, ye angels that have voice! Oh! help my nothingness, Thou Spirit all-creating, Thou that givest beauty to the void, and form to shapeless chaos!

Oh! what did I behold? There was a pillar there within the open court. They dragged my Master there. They stripped Him of His robe. His blessed arms they rudely strained, and bound them far above His head. And when I saw His shoulders bare, His back exposed before the angry crowd, His virgin flesh for sinful eyes to look upon, for sinful hands to touch, my life seemed sinking far away, my heart refused to beat. "O my Jesus!" did I sob. "This sight is far too much for me. Thy poor and feeble child will die. He is not living now." And then there came a love within my soul that seemed to take the place of life. It was only love. It was not I. This is the flesh of my Beloved! This is the food of virgin hearts. This is the bread by which the pure shall live.

Then, while my heart exulted in the thought that this dear flesh of Mary's Child was mine, and heaven's wide windows opened to my longing gaze, where virgins walked in raiment white with lilies crowned, I saw the ruffian arms uplifted to their utmost strength, and heard the blows which fell with leaden weight. They ploughed great seams upon His back; they tore His flesh with thongs that bared the bone. His mangled shoulders were like many cruel wounds, one sightless mass of curdling blood. He bent beneath the fearful pain. I could not see His face. His head was bowed. I saw Him tremble as His hands held fast the ropes, and fierce convulsions, like the struggles dire of death with manhood's strength, were shaking all His frame, until his tottering limbs gave way. I saw Him turn as white as is the icy coldness of the dead, and then as red as blood which streamed with feverish heat from bruised and mangled veins. I know not how I looked. Some mighty power then held me there and forced my eyes; I could not turn away. So, like the corpse that cannot move, whose glassy eyes are fixed and seem to stare on vacancy, my sightless orbs were hanging on the scene. Was I fainting, dying there? Oh! it was far more. Did I see or did I feel? I know my Master fell; I heard a groan. I saw His bleeding back, His face as white as death, and then I knew no more. There came an awful sickness at my heart, where every pulse was still and sight and sense were gone. I was falling, falling as in endless depths. Would there never come a pause? Must I sink eternally? And then when ages seemed to pass and I was sinking still, my feet were resting on some solid base, and I was running, running on, so wearied I could scarcely stand, and yet I ran. Some power unseen was driving me with limbs exhausted and with panting breath. Oh! can I never stop? I cried. Then afar, where distance seemed impassable, the bleeding form of my Beloved ran before me. The pillar moved as fast as He. The mangled shoulders shone like light. I was travelling in the might no force of mine could disobey, and still so far before me moved the deathlike face. I was losing step by step my strength. At last I sobbed: "O my Jesus, loving, bleeding Master! do not fly from me! Oh! let me come. I am dying now. I must not die away from Thee." And then I fell indeed. It was not sleep; it was not death. One sense alone remained; and was it sight? For, burning in my brain like fire that melts the metals in their strength, there was the pillar and the scourge, the gashed and mangled back, the trembling frame, the swollen eyes of my Beloved.

Then, if I had thought, the thought was prayer. I called my Master by His dearest names. I wrestled with myself that I might speak. There was no voice while love was in my heart like flame, a love that sought the pinioned arms, that nestled in the point of thong and scourge, and rested on the naked breast.

Before me ran the precious blood. It was the stream of life. Is this the heaven where crystal waters glide, where sparkling waves like gems reflect the uncreated light? Oh! no, this cannot be, for here is pain, and here is grief, and here the shadow of the cross! Yet rest awhile and bathe within this stream, and thou shalt see how every shadow falls, how every stain is washed away, how white and pure thy hands and heart shall be. And then it seemed that I was not alone. I woke to sounds so soft and sweet that fear was passing from my soul, and joy was coming with my tears. How can I smile? I cried; how can my heart be glad amid these awful scenes? Where, oh! where is my Beloved gone? I cannot see Him now. The pillar and the scourge are vanished, too. If you are angels come to guide my sorrowing steps, then lead me after Him. I must be sad; I cannot now rejoice! Then came a strain of song celestial from unearthly harps—a song so full of sadness sweet, and yet so mighty in its power, that I was borne along upon its gentle tide, and peace like that of heaven was sinking in my troubled heart. Surely these are messengers of light. They are the angels of the King. How came they here within these caverns drear? What canticles of grace are sounding now? There passed before my eyes a vision blest of saints in glad array with glittering crowns and raiment white. They were marching on and moving to the song. There were virgins then with lilies pure upon their heads. There were martyrs wearing crimson robes and bearing in their hands the palm. And pontiffs led the priestly train, as on their ranks the cross was shining like a golden sun. The long procession moved before me like the pageant of a prince upon his coronation day. I heard the words of their celestial song, as spirits leading on were filling all the air with melody. "Come virgins pure, come spouses of the Lamb, come to the crowning of the King. Lift up the notes of minstrelsy divine. Sing, Cherubim and Seraphim, before the throne."

And I was moving on with them. My feeble tongue, unloosed, was joining in the strain; and rapture like the ecstasy of heaven was stealing o'er my powers. How can I chant this wondrous song? How can my lips awake the notes of joy? Where is my bleeding King? where is the pillar now? where is the throne? Oh! where shall

He be crowned on this His dying day? And yet my voice went on, as if an angel touched my mouth and words unbidden came: "Come virgins pure, come spouses of the Lamb, come to the crowning of the King."

Was this the vision which my precious Master gave my fainting soul to cheer me in my sorrowing way? Oh! did His mercy open then mine eyes that I might see, and by the sight be strengthened when the deeper darkness fell? I only know that suddenly the awful transformation came. The light went out; the music ceased; the angels passed away; the virgin train was gone. And I was standing all alone. And then instead of heavenly harps I heard the clash of arms, the jeers of human voices coarse. "Behold the King," they cried. "Come bow before Him here. The Nazarene is sitting here in regal state. Behold the purple robe he wears, the sceptre in his hand, the crown upon His head. This is the royal prince of David's line." And then foul curses rent the air with laughing mockery. How came I here? The spirits pure were guiding me. Is this the throne of Mary's Child and God's eternal Son? Is this the coronation-day the angels' songs were telling of when I was moving to the tune of their celestial strains? O, my Master dear! lift up my face and let me look on Thee. If this be really Thou, my God, my All, why cease the seraphs' notes, and where are gone the spouses of the Prince, the glories of Thy virgin train? Why is this Thy feeble child alone amid the ribald jests and oaths of blasphemy? He gave me strength to raise mine eyes, where once again I saw His blessed face. He even looked at me and smiled. I saw him sitting on a bag of straw. There was a worn and tattered purple rag around his shoulders bruised and bare. In His right hand He held a reed. Upon His royal head there was a crown of thorns. The thorns were sharp and long. I saw the soldiers strike it with their spears. I saw the look of pain that forced the blood from every point. I saw the swollen eyes from which the tears ran down. I saw Him tremble as the anguish grew with every blow. "Oh! indeed," cried I, "this is the crowning of the King. He is the King of heaven and all the earth; He is the Master of my soul. But oh! is this His coronation-day? And is He thus arrayed, the heavenly purple torn aside, the reed of straw the sceptre of the eternal Son, the only crown a diadem of thorns? O my Prince! is this the crown Thy children give? Is this the throne prepared for Thee on earth?" And then my love went up to Him with prayer, with all the incense of my heart. "O my Jesus!" sighed my soul, "if this indeed be now Thy coronation-hour, if this Thy chosen regal state, then bid the angels come again, and tune my voice that I may sing Thy praise."

Alas! the heavenly harps were still. There was no response. I know not how I drew so near, but I was kneeling at His feet. "Dear, precious feet," I sighed, "now you are mine again. My Master, how I love Thee, how I worship Thee with all the powers of thought or soul! Rule my every faculty and be in truth my King! Reign for ever, Prince of peace, and in the glory of Thy kingdom come!"

Alas! my peace was short; the bliss of touching Him soon passed, and I was rudely torn away. The ruffians came once more to beat Him with their hands, to spit upon His swollen face, to press the agonizing crown upon His temples gashed and raw, to mock His tears, to strike Him with His reed of straw.

Then how I prayed, while deadly faintness came, and all my sight was gone. There was no sense, yet fast within my brain in lines of fire I felt the picture of my thorn-crowned King. "O Master dear! I die to all but Thee. Canst Thou speak to me again before they drag Thee to Thy cross? This is, I know, the day of Thine espousals pure. For virgin souls the heavenly Bridegroom comes. For them He wears the crown upon His head divine. For them it is a crown that bleeds. I can hardly live, I love Thee so. The springs of life are nearly quenched to see Thee in the pain the nuptial garment brings. From every piercing point there is a drop of blood for me. Why dost Thou tremble so, my blessed One? Too heavy is the burden Thou art bearing now! Oh! do not faint again. Thy loving child is near to death. If Thou dost fall upon Thy throne, then he will die indeed!"

My spirit seemed to pass away from earth, but not from Him. He was near me all the while, and soon when shadowy forms were crowding round, and faces of the dead were staring full on me, I heard His voice. It was weak—alas! how weak—and yet, like whisper faint, it roused my every sense. O the precious hour! I cannot lose a word. This is the message from my King. It is His coronation-day:

"My child, thy Bridegroom is indeed a King. The diadems of heaven by right are His. Where Cherubim and Seraphim are bowing down, beyond the sea of glass, He sits upon the eternal throne. Yet hath He taken thy humanity for love of thee, that He may reign as man and make His loving heart the centre of His sway. So must He lead the souls He seeks to purify where earth shall lose its charms, where pride shall die. There is no earthly crown that He could wear upon His head divine. The gems the world adores reflect alone created light. What is that light to Him who is the brightness of the Father's face, who is the sun of the celestial sphere? He cometh to atone for sin, to pay the debt for all the fallen race, to wash with blood the stains no fount but that which springeth from His veins could cleanse. The children born of Him must crown Him with their hands, and He must bleed from every thorn, that all their sins of thought and foolish pride may rest upon His royal head, that in His anguish fierce all human love may die, and all the springs of thought and will be purified.

"Behold Me, then, a thorn-crowned

King. I rule by pain. I suffer for the pride of those I love. It is a struggle long, a battle dire to conquer each rebellious foe, that those who choose Me for their spouse may thus be truly one with Me in heart and will; that all self-love shall cease; that they may have no thought but Mine. I am their King; they call Me Master dear, but every moment they are pressing thorns upon My brow. Sometimes they glory in My gifts as if their own; sometimes they seek to lead me in their ways; sometimes refuse to follow patiently My steps; sometimes they pride themselves upon the pledges of My heart, the ring I put upon their hand, the cross they wear upon their breast. And then, forgetful of the jealous God whose eyes are open everywhere, they offer incense to self-will, and blindly turn away in paths unblest and wander far from Me. The love of creatures they have crucified, while love of self is poisoning all their life. They enter on the way of saints, but cannot die to live, or sink to nothingness that thus, indeed, their heavenly Spouse may reign alone. And so they press the sharpened points upon My head, and I must feel the hurt which breaks My heart. They cannot love Me for Myself, or they forget that I am God, whose wisdom hath no bounds, who could not fail to guide aright His chosen souls. I cannot lead them to the pastures of My choice; I cannot fold them to My breast; I cannot kiss them with My lips. They only touch the thorns. They wound themselves and Me. I am wrestling with them all their lives. They are ever hurting Me, ever pressing down My crown of pain. I cannot purify their thoughts. I cannot kill desires, cannot make them all My own.

"Could I tell you, O My loving child!

how glad I am to wear this crown? It is the secret of My sway o'er hearts that bleed. It is the sign of heavenly life where nature dies. And yet the pain is known to God alone. Did ever bridegroom struggle with his bride, or lover with the loved, as I must wrestle with the chosen souls who call Me Spouse? The pride of all the earth, the root of every sin, every rent of this My seamless robe, every wound upon My body mystical, are thorns within My crown. Oh! how My temples ache; oh! how the brain is burning as with thousand fires; oh! the agony untold of this My coronation-day. And yet the thorns that hurt Me most are those that come from loving hands, from those who call Me Bridegroom dear, from those who seek to honor Me. I ask their hearts, their souls, their minds, their strength. They cannot even see how every thought of infidelity is hurting Me. I want them at My side; I want them on My breast; I yearn to clasp them closely with Mine arms, that they may look on Me, and I may let them see, indeed, the face of their Beloved in all His winning charms. They will not come. They stand afar. They seem afraid to touch My hand. I know it bleeds, but bleeding is the sign of love. Ah! no; I must endure this pain. Oh! let the thorns go down. It will ease My heart to suffer all the sharpest pangs for them. When they have wounded Me enough, then they may learn the tenderness of their Beloved, and they may feel what might have been the fondness of My sweet caress, if they had not repulsed Me with a cold neglect. Who are they that never touched My crown, who never gave Me pain? Their names are written here within My heart. They shall walk with Me in white. They have passed

before Me in the glittering train. With
angels they have come to chant their
coronation-song. They are the children
of the Queen, the spotless Mother of
her God. To her I owe this bright array, for she hath taught to virgin souls
how Mary's child can love.

"And now you hear the blessed name
of the Immaculate. Go meet her as she
comes. Go pray to her for grace to
know the riches of the heart that
calleth you from every earthly tie. Go
kneel where she shall kneel. Go look
upon her blessed face and put your
hands in hers. Then let Me rest awhile
upon this throne of straw, here gather
up My strength that I may tread the
weary road, that I may take My cross
and bear it to the hill of sacrifice. I
see the painful path, the cleft within
the rock, the mouldering skulls, the
open grave."

When thus my Master spoke I shuddered at the words, while faintness seized upon my heart. I bowed my face upon the earth, and prayed for grace to feel the thorns my wilful pride had pressed upon His head. If I might feel the pain, or even share the anguish I had brought on Him, it seemed I might repent, that I might love Him more, and never once again be base enough to wound Him so. Too well my daring prayer found answer on this dreadful day. The faintness I had felt grew like the agony of death. My pulses ceased, my limbs grew cold. Sharp pangs like thorns were piercing down my brain, and every point seemed like a tongue of fire. It was no earthly fire. I knew of pain that in its dire excess uplifts the reason from her seat and hangs the tortured frame upon the border-line of life. Yet this was more. My head seemed shut within a vise of iron heated hot, and then some mighty hand was forcing down the burning points. And with this awful agony there came a fear that seemed more direful than the thorns. Oh! had I grieved again my Master dear? Had I presumed to ask for pain? Was one like me so bold to come where angels are afraid? Oh! could I touch the footprints of my Love, or dare to put my hands upon His crown? I could do much if He were there to hold me up! If He, my strength, were gone one second from my sight, then surely I should faint and fall. And now where is my Love? I see Him not. I cannot even feel. Here was the throne of straw, and here the King was crowned, and here He spoke to me! And now the thorns are killing me, and I am left alone! Alas! some fearful dream is passing o'er my brain, and when I wake, my soul shall be aroused to sorrows new. Is this, indeed, the day of doom? What makes me tremble so, and why am I so cold? The grave itself can never be like this!

O Master dear, my King! I cried. Show me Thy face once more. Oh! tell me, is Thy trial ended now?

As suddenly as light the scene was changed. The palace-walls were once again before mine eyes. The crowd was surging round the court. Coarse voices shouted long and loud: "Let Him be crucified!" "Let Cæsar's rival die! The Roman Cæsar is our king. This is the Nazarene. Command Him to the cross. Upon the hill of skulls let Him be crucified." And then I raised my eyes, and there He stood upon the mighty portico of Pilate's hall. He stood before the furious mob, before the priests in full array, before the soldiers with their spears, before the Roman governor, who seemed to fear to speak. His hands were bound, the purple robe was on His breast, the crown of thorns was on His head. His face was bowed, His eyes cast down. He seemed so weak that death was surely nigh. And yet the majesty of God was clothing Him as if with light from heaven. I heard the Roman say: "Behold the Man." "Behold your King." And then I heard again the angry clamor rise: "Great Cæsar is our king." "Let Him, the Nazarene, be crucified." Then while I looked and loved, as I had never loved before, I seemed to catch the notes of some celestial song which, far above the sinful noise of earth, was sounding in the skies: "Indeed behold the Man, the Virgin's Child, the Word made flesh, the Adam of the new and living race. All worthy is the Lamb that dies. Upon His royal head be honor, wisdom, strength. To Him let every creature bow from heaven's eternal arch to earth's remotest bound.

To Him who sitteth on the throne be adoration paid. This is the Son of God. Sing, ye choirs of spirits blest; come sing His everlasting reign."·* These heavenly notes a moment cheered my drooping soul. The clouds that gathered round My Love in bonds, an instant broke in light, and rays of uncreated brilliancy were beaming on my Master's bowed but royal head.

Yet soon the song had ceased, the light was gone, the cloud returned, the darkness grew apace.

There was an awful moment then. The soldiers heard the voice of Pilate there, and stood with their uplifted spears. In trembling tones he spoke: "Behold the Nazarene. You ask His life. I see no cause why He should die. I hear your witnesses in vain. I know your accusations false. And yet you will not rest until you lead Him to a

* Apocalypse v. 8-13.

shameful death. In Cæsar's name you ask the cross. In Cæsar's regal state, against my will, against the voice of right, o'erwhelmed with many fears, I grant your wish. His blood shall rest on you and all your guilty race. I shall pronounce the fearful doom that sinks the glory of your land, the coming of your endless night. I sentence unto death your King. Behold Him crowned with thorns. Go take Him to the cross and lead Him off to Golgotha. Between the malefactors let Him die. Yet shall He wear in death the title of a prince, and from the cruel gibbet reign. Let the trumpets blow. Throughout the Roman's wide domain announce His doom."

There was an instant's pause. My heart was sinking in the depths of fear and grief and shame, and every struggling breath was love or prayer. The soldiers seized my precious Lord;

with hands so rude they tore the purple robe away. They threw the reed upon the ground. They brought the seamless garment which His Mother made, and on His bleeding shoulders clothed Him once again. With cruel violence they pressed the thorns upon His brow. They bound Him with their ropes around His waist, and as the Roman trumpets blew they dragged Him on. The sun was rising to its noon, and yet the sky was like the coming of a fearful storm, or as the shadows that precede the night. I heard the tramp of arms, the shouts that rose on every side like voices from the depths of hell. I saw the sad procession move. They led the way to Calvary. Their spears were pointing to the hill. My Blessed Lord was passing from my sight. I fell upon my knees. I kissed the ground His feet had blessed. I ran before the crowd, and as they pushed Him rudely on I bowed before Him with a yearning heart. "Jesus, Master, let me go with Thee. Where art Thou guiding now Thy broken-hearted child? I will follow in Thy steps, and like burning flames to Thee my love shall rise. Thy footprints crimsoned with Thy blood will I adore." He turned and smiled on me; and oh! for all eternity my heart shall treasure up that smile. His face was sad and pale. His eyes were full of tears. His precious lips were trembling as He seemed to say: "I am condemned to death. Now let Me look on thee. Art thou indeed My spouse? Then pray for grace. I go before thee with My staff and rod. The clouds shall cover thee in gloom. The waters cold shall swallow thee with Me. The mountain-tops shall fall, the earth shall quake. The prince of fear shall reign. Yet come, My loving child! The Bridegroom leads the sorrowing way. The Spirit bids the bride to come."

MEDITATION EIGHTH.

THE WAY TO CALVARY.

MEDITATION EIGHTH.

THE WAY TO CALVARY.

"I sleep, and my heart watcheth: the voice of my Beloved knocking: Open to me, my sister, my love, my dove, my undefiled: for my head is full of dew, and my locks of the drops of the night."—CANTICLES v. 2.

My soul was sad. I heard my Master tell of sadness unto death, when in the garden He endured the sharpness of His woe, when there the shades of sorrow covered Him, while thus the heart divine was broken with the grief. I only touched the border of the cloud. My feeble sight could only see the outline of the shadow dense and drear. The little life I had seemed lost in Him, and pangs of superhuman pain were blinding every sense. Yet there in all the awful night my Blessed Love was nigh. And I was watching then; and if my tears were flowing fast, my weeping was for Him.

But now the fear of parting comes. The end draws near. The precious Master of my soul will die! I know that He must die. This fearful hour has been my dread. The hour has come! The altar is in sight. The Victim hastens there. The hill of Calvary frowns before mine eyes. I see the cross. I see the sad yet willing face of my Beloved. He goes to death as bridegroom to the bridal halls. He bids me follow in His steps. The Spirit bids the bride to come. How can I go and see Him die, and then be left alone? He told me that the earth should quake, the sun should hide his face, the dead in ghostly shapes arise. Such darkness has no gloom for me. But when He dies indeed, how can I live? How can I bear the loneliness when I shall kneel beneath the body of my sacred dead, when Calvary's shades shall hide the light of earth and heaven? How can I bear this parting from my Love?

And yet I cannot choose but go. I cannot leave Him while He lives, and if I die with Him my grateful soul shall bless the hour. It is not death I fear, surely not a death with Him. I only fear I cannot live until He dies. The silver cord may break too soon. The cloud may blind my eyes and paralyze my sense. I may not see Him die. I may not catch His parting glance. He may not bid farewell to me, or give me once again the smile I love so well. Yet must I go. My heart is weak. My limbs are trembling with my grief. Indeed, the waters touch my aching feet. I need His staff and rod. While He will bear the heavy cross, He still can carry me. Jesus, Master, Love, I come!

Lead Thou me on. Put out Thine hands divine, and I am strong.

And I am travelling now the weary, sorrowing road, the way that leads to Calvary. So treading in my Bridegroom's steps I journey on; falling, rising, fainting, weeping, I am moving on. It is not I. The self I knew is gone. I only know one life, and in that life I see and hear and feel. The Spirit moves my helpless hands and feet. The Spirit guides my eyes. The Blessed Spirit teaches me the riches of my Love, unfolds the graces of my Master dear, and shows to me the beauties of His dying face, the depths of pity infinite that draws me to His bleeding arms. O mighty Spirit, eternal in Thy reign! come help me in this path of pain. Come touch my eyes that they may see. Come touch my lips that they may speak.

I saw my Jesus standing in the court. The sad procession stays a moment there.

Dread silence reigns where curse and jeer were sounding on the air. They bring the heavy cross—the sacred wood for which He sighed, the blessed tree that bears the fruit of life. Alas! its awful weight will crush His wasted frame. It is His burden dear; the sins of all the world are resting there. With rudeness vile, with cruel haste, they lay it on His shoulders gashed and bleeding from the scourge. He staggers helplessly; He trembles fearfully. He can hardly bear the weight. His blessed face turns icy pale. He gasps for breath. He nearly falls. He almost bends unto the ground. The edges sharp are opening wide the seams upon His back. He lifts His weary hands. With loving smile He holds the crushing burden as He tries to walk. The blood is flowing down. It runs upon His arms and hands; it falls upon the ground. He moves with pain. At every step the weight seems killing Him. His face is like the face of death.

O my loving Lord beneath this burden dire, how can I comfort Thee, how share the heavy sorrows of Thy cross? I saw Him fainting, moving slowly on. How can He walk to Calvary? Surely He will die before the sacred hill be reached. I followed in His steps. I did not hear the rabble cry. The soldiers marched along with spears uplifted and the sound of arms. I did not hear their words. There was a silence deep within my soul. I heard His sighs, I saw Him bending 'neath the awful load. His face was full of sweetness as He looked to heaven or turned to me. And oh! the sadness of His eyes divine was more than flesh could bear. My heart was begging Him to speak one word. I knew my sins were bearing on His shoulders then. I knew that I was crushing down my only Love, that He was taking up my cross. My lips were murmuring words of prayer, as sadness unto death was filling all my soul. O Master dear! I see my sins upon Thee now. The weight I could not bear is laid on Thee. Oh! canst Thou love me still? I have not only wounded Thee, but here upon Thy bleeding back I see the awful load of all my crimes, of my untruth to Thee. Am I, Thy bride, to grieve and hurt the Bridegroom so? And did I call Thee Love, and thus afflict Thee with my faithless, wayward heart? Alas! I cannot bear to see Thee tremble so beneath the weight of my ingratitude! Tell me, Master dear, oh! canst Thou love me still?

He turned and looked on me a moment then. His precious face seemed very near to mine. I felt the breath which struggling came as He essayed to speak. There was a look of love, like that I saw in Pilate's hall when sorrowing Peter came. I was so drawn to touch Him then that I had given worlds to kiss His wearied feet. I know not if I knelt, for I was moving slowly on with Him, almost as faint as He, and straining all my senses to the whisper of His voice.

"O my precious child! dost Thou ask Me if I love Thee now? Is not this the proof of love? Dost thou not know that I must bear thy cross, that I must teach thee how to walk the weary road, that I must lead the way where spouses of My choice must follow Me? All My Loves are led to Calvary. There, and only there, the lights of earth grow dim; there, and only there, I rule the chastened soul, and make the bridal hour the hour of sacrifice. Thy sins have hurt Me where My bursting heart is bleeding fast. They open wide the seams of scourge and thong. But I am God, and when the crushing load is breaking Me I set thee free. I bear thy griefs, and thou art Mine. Thus God alone can tell the riches of forgiving love, or know how dear becomes the sinner ransomed by My blood, made pure by grace, and nourished at My breast. Oh! let thy love renew its power to see the awful cost of thine espousals to the King of saints, the King that lays His heavenly purple down, that tracks His steps in blood beneath the cross, to celebrate in death the nuptial rite, to bind the soul forgiven to His everlasting arms, to give the sweet embrace of love divine. Faint not, my child. I suffer awful pangs for thee; I love thee for the pain I bear. It is the sealing of the eternal bond. Thou art born to Me in agony. Thou comest from My open side. Thou art the child of Calvary. Press onward to thy home."

I cannot tell how near my Master

then became to me. His arms, which bore the cross, seemed twining round my breast. I thought I felt the beating of His heart in union strange, to me before unknown. I knew He loved me then. In sorrow far too deep for mortal tongue, my heart was glad with joy that lifted me in ecstasy above the scenes of time. I turned my tearful eyes to heaven. I felt the angels near. I tried to think of Father, Son, and Spirit blest on their eternal seat of light; and clouds of golden hue were passing like the vast procession of the saints and massing round the throne. I thought I saw my Master there arrayed in glorious might. The cross was there all glittering as the sun at noon. The hands and feet were wounded, too; the breast was opened wide. Where had I wandered, then? Surely this is not the weary road. There is no Calvary's mountain here. Was I pressing onward to my home?

Was I selfish, then, to wander so? I had no choice. Some hand unseen was guiding me, that I was not the master of my will. I only thought of Him. I never for an instant lost the sight of Jesus bowed beneath the cross, bending, fainting, weeping, struggling on.

So suddenly an awful faintness seized my heart. The light above was gone. It was the height of noon, and yet there came the dimness of the night. The sharpness of a pain before unfelt awoke me to my sight. My blessed Lord had ceased to move. His face had changed. His eyes are fixed. His feet are paralyzed. His hands have fallen from the cross. His head was drooping on His breast. Oh! He will fall beneath that weight and die. "Help, angels, help! O Michael, mighty prince! come in thy strength. Come, Gabriel, in thy gentle ministry. Come, Raphael, healer of the weak. Come, ye powers that rule the spheres! The Son of God will fall and dash His feet against the stones. O my Mother! art thou coming now? My Master told me thou wouldst come. He bade me pray to thee and ask to put my hands in thine. O glorious Queen! where art thou now? My failing eyes are seeking thee. Come to take thy Child within thine arms ere He shall die."

Alas! it is too late. My Love has fallen as if dead. Prostrate on the ground He lies. The heavy cross is crushing Him. He cannot move. I can scarcely see Him breathe. Oh! how stiff and cold He lies! His beauteous face is whiter than the snow. His glassy eyes are fixed. There is no motion; but the tears are slowly running down, and drops of blood are trickling from the thorns which pierce His head anew. "O my Jesus! let me come and touch Thee now with all the tenderness of love. Thou art not dead, I know, for here are not the skulls, and this is not the hill of sacrifice. Our parting has not come. Thou hast fainted with the grievous load, but Thou wilt rise again. Let me help Thee, Master dear. I am so faint myself that I can hardly breathe, yet I could give the little strength I have to Thee."

I never prayed as I prayed then. I had no life but prayer, yet had I poorly counted all the cost. When I was pressing on, and holding out my hands that I might only touch the wearied feet, as there so cold they lay upon the ground, my tottering limbs refused my will, and I fell prostrate by my Master's side. At last, I said, the hour has come. This is my death, and all is over now. There is no Calvary for me. I have no strength. Alas! how weak I am! Oh! must all my hopes be buried here? There is no cross upon my shoulders now, and yet I faint and die!

How long endured my seeming death I do not know. From faintness to unconsciousness I struggled on, and when my senses woke my ears were startled by the sounds I heard in Pilate's court. There were curses loud. There were blows. They were beating as before my precious Love. They were bidding Him to rise with oaths profane. Where was I, then? I thought the trial scene was passed. I thought the soldiers led Him down the hill. I surely saw the cross upon His bleeding shoulders as He fell.

Awake, my soul! awake to see and hear. Bid every sense arouse. The Mother of the King is coming now in all her grace to aid your feebleness. The Queen of Sorrows rules on Calvary. You could not move without her help. No soul can watch upon the mountain drear, unless she hide him in her mantle pure, and hold his hands amid the phantoms of the grave where Jesus lies.

There came a gentle ray upon my utter darkness then, and my unconsciousness was passing like the shadows at the dawn. There came a peace within my soul, and scales were falling from my eyes. I knew the source of all this blessed light. I saw the beauteous form of her I love with all my heart for Jesus' sake. She is my Mother dear. I owe my life to her. She did put her hand upon my darkened eyes, did win me by her gentleness, did lead me to her Child, and teach me how to love my God. O Mother of my soul! thou art coming now in this my dire distress. I will take thee to my prostrate Lord. See, here He lies as faint and weak as death, and yet I know He is not dead. Oh! come, my Mother, with thy angels bright. Bring Gabriel ever at thy side. We will draw near my dying Love, and if thy precious hands shall touch Him He will rise. The priceless days of Bethlehem and Nazareth come back to Him beneath His cross. Thy loving arms shall once again assuage His tears and fold Him to thy breast. I ran with eager haste, with all the confidence of Mary's child. But oh! how changed that dear and gentle face! She came upon the scene with all the grandeur of a queen. The Magdalen was weeping at her side, and John was guiding her with loving words. I could not hear his voice. He trembled as he tried to hold her up, while his pure eyes were full of tears. The Virgin stood as if the clouds were rolling 'neath her feet, as if she stood on space, with air of majesty to reign. She moved with fixed and eager gaze. In every line and feature sorrow spoke, the sorrow which is unto death. The glowing beauty of the skies was covered with a pall. The eyes that seemed like mirrors of the heavenly light were red with tears, and opened wide as if to see some horrid, crushing sight. Her hands so white and fair were folded on her breast, as if to hold the heart that ached and struggled with her grief. Oh! cried I in utter woe, what can I do? How can I bear the crucifixion of my Lord, and of His Mother too? Then, ever gentle as the heart from which she draws her grace, she looked at me and motioned me to come. She seemed to say: "My chosen child, the lover of my Jesus dear, come here to me. I see the ring upon thy hand. I see the marks upon thy brow. Art thou the spouse of my Beloved, who here has called thee to the nuptial rite? Dost thou love Him with all thy soul? Is He in truth thy Bridegroom pure? Then come and take my hand. My Son has told me of thy name. He bade me lead thee here where flesh must fail. Thou must weep with me. I am a victim at this altar, too, but I will hold thee up within the awful night. And thou shalt keep with me the vigil drear, the fearful watch on Calvary. Come near me, child. I love thee with a mother's tenderness. Thy griefs are mine, and we are one, for Jesus is our all. But oh! the sword is piercing now my very soul. Pray, pray with all your strength, and leave me not a moment here. Together we shall go this road of sorrows that shall break the heart of God and mine. When my hand grows cold, then hold it fast.

When I tremble fearfully, as if to die, then be thou brave and show thy love. See here, my Jesus calls! He rises from the ground, so pale, so weak. He looks at me through tears with love I know full well. It is my God whom I adore. It is my Child, my very flesh and blood. I must go to Him; come thou with me."

I turned to follow her, and then indeed my constancy was tried. My Master, risen from His swoon beneath the cross, was seeking her with eyes that spoke a tenderness no mortal tongue can tell. I never saw Him look as then. His face was paler than the dead. His hands so weak were feeling for the cross. It seemed as if His feet were swollen and His limbs were paralyzed. He staggered as He stood, and as the bleeding shoulders bent to take again the cruel load. The blood was trickling down His arms and hands, and running from the thorny crown. The royal brow was marked with many wounds. The hair was clotted with the mire and blood, while spittle still defiled the beauty of His face. Then as one dead, and yet the Prince of life, He stood, as if He held the angel back until His hour should come.

The piteous look He gave was more than I could bear. I hid mine eyes beneath the mantle of my Queen, and sobbed with her. Her precious hand grew cold indeed. I held it fast, but mine was like the ice, and yet I clasped with all my strength the fingers dear that so entwined themselves in mine. She trembled like the flowers that break before the storm and scatter to the winds of heaven. Convulsions like the agonies of death were shaking every limb, while sighs were coming from her panting breast, and tears were flowing like the rain. Surely, Mother dear, I cried, your hour has come. You cannot live to see this sight. Where, then, shall hide your helpless child? O blessed Queen! I cannot let thee die. We must wait until He dies. He cannot go alone to Calvary. You must lead me there, and teach me how to kneel beneath the cross.

She sprang from me as if for life. Oh! let me go, she cried. This is my place. Oh! let me touch my Son once more. I must soothe His pain with my caress. My hands shall ease the anguish He endures, and gently touch the gaping wounds of scourge and thorn and cross. My kiss shall wipe the tears away, and I will take the spittle and the mire. It will give Him strength to feel the pressure of my lips. He is my own, my babe of Bethlehem. This flowing blood is mine. These eyes are mine. These swollen lips are mine. I am a mother now, and

I will go to Him. No spear nor sword shall keep me from my Child. I care not for the curse or oath. I care not for their cruel violence to me. My mother's heart is bleeding now. There is no creature love like mine.

My dearest Mother ran from me, but all in vain. I saw my Jesus lift His tearful face, and all the love of heaven was beaming in His swollen eyes. This is the glance which makes the bliss of saints. It spoke to her who knew its meaning well; and she, who treasured every change upon the face divine, saw how the heart of God was hers by ties before unknown. And this was more than all the kisses of His mouth. It told of deeper love than all the childhood's happy hours. Though held by rude and ruffian hands, yet was she nearer to her Child than when He nestled in her fond embrace.

Oh! how I loved my Master then, as

thus I saw His heart revealed and saw in that exchange of tenderness the Mother and the Son.

She feasted on that glance. She read its lesson well, and then, with hands outstretched, she sprang to hold Him to her breast. Her lips were moving to the words, "My Son, my God, Thy loving Mother comes." And then I saw the soldiers turn their spears and push her back. I saw the crowd rush in with rudeness coarse. She seemed in agony that robs the sense of life. She neither heard nor saw. I know not if she felt. For like a corpse she fell upon the ground, while there the furious rabble closed around, and with an oath they forced my Jesus on.

They beat Him with their whips as then He struggled to obey. He saw His Mother fall, and bent beneath the cross as if some awful pang was piercing Him anew. I never saw Him look so sad, not even in the garden's shade when, holding with His hands His heart, He wept like one bereft of all. He looked upon the fallen form of her He held so dear, and turned His face away, while sobs seemed stifling Him and tears were flowing like the rain. For once He lifted up His eyes to heaven; then, looking forward to the hill of Calvary, He staggered on.

I knelt beside my blessed Mother's side, and wept and prayed. Oh! how beautiful she seemed in her sad death. I kissed her cold and helpless hands. I called her by her dearest name. I begged the spirits of the light to come. I asked for Raphael's healing power. I prayed that Gabriel's soothing hands might touch her prostrate form; for well I knew that she must rise, that she must stand on Golgotha and there teach me to watch, and there receive the dying glances of her Child.

The crowd passed on and we were left alone. Some gentle air of paradise like life divine seemed coming then. I felt the presence of the angels there, and bowed my head in praise. She moved at last. The sighs came pouring from her breast. She loosed her hands from mine and laid them on her heart. She moved her lips in prayer. I heard her ask for strength. "O Jesus dear, my Child! Thy Mother's heart is pierced indeed. Many are the shadows I have seen; Thy chalice drear has been my portion, too, but now the end is near. The cross shall hold us both. Thy weary way is mine. Thy nails shall pierce my hands and feet. The spear that touches Thee shall find its home within my breast. I tell it not to angels drooping at my side. The Cherubim can wonder at my woe, but Thou alone, my God, canst read my agony. For far above all finite powers.

my grief is hidden in the love I have for Thee, the love the seraph's bright intelligence may praise, the love which no created intellect may know. O Jesus mine! as we were ever one, so now the deeper bond shall bind us fast for all eternity. The cross shall be our tie, the wounds within Thy precious hands and feet and opened breast, the seals of union strange, before impossible. The drops of blood that fall upon Thy Mother now shall lift her up beyond the sea of glass. I answer to Thy grace, my Child. I am coming now! I will not fall again. The spear already in my heart shall there abide. Forgive my tears, forget my sighs. The sorrowing Mother comes to take her place. She will be with Thee unto the last. Her truth shall be Thy rest when all things fail. The incense of her heart shall rise to Thee when angels' harps are mute. Her love shall linger on Thy passing breath and speed Thy spirit to its home above. Her hands shall yet embrace her Child in death, and leave Him in the silent tomb. O Love divine! assist me now; the Queen of Martyrs comes."

So when my precious Mother spoke these words there came a calm upon her agonizing face. She raised her head, while light unearthly shone upon her features pale. Her eyes, so like her Child's, were looking straight to heaven, as if this earth with all its scenes had passed away. She rose, but not alone. I knew the angels of her train were at her side. In worship high, in reverential fear, I bowed and blessed the spirits of the heavenly court who came at her command. "O Mary, Mother blest! the seraphs come to greet thee in thy passion's hour. Their arms shall hold thee up; their wings of light sustain the Mother of their God. Yet canst thou look on me again so feebly kneeling here, thou Queen of all the hosts above? While I am here, so little and so low, the angels move obedient to thy will. Oh! may I touch thy hand again and tell thee of my love? And will the glorious Queen of Heaven now guide my steps, and lead me on, and teach me how to keep my vigil drear among the skulls, in nature's dire eclipse, beneath the cross?"

I turned my trembling face. The Virgin stood as on a cloud which angels held beneath her feet. She looked at me and smiled through tears. It seemed as if my Jesus smiled, so closely did her face resemble His. All His beauty, all His gentleness, and all His grace were in that smile. She gave her precious hand to me. She clasped my hand in hers. "My child," she said, "how little you can know the heart of your Beloved in all its wealth of tenderness! You cannot even know how dear to me are souls espoused by Him, or how the torrent of His love o'erflows within my breast. I cherish you because you are His spouse, because you wear His nature too. Your features, too, redeemed and washed in blood, are like to His. The seraph's nature He did not espouse. Below the ranks of spirits blest He stooped to be my Son, to die and live for you. I see His marks upon your brow. I see in you my own, my Jesus as He lives in you. Come, then, with me. My broken heart shall be your guide. The Victim of the cross is moving on, and Calvary's hill is frowning at us there. The hour of crucifixion comes. The knell of death is sounding in my ears."

And then the cloud that seemed to rest beneath her feet moved slowly down the steep descent. I held her trembling hand and hid myself within her mantle's folds. The blessed John was walking at her side as if with painful steps, and Magdalen transfixed with fear, as if the fountains of her blood were frozen in her breast. Then, when we reached the foot of the descent and saw the path that climbs to Calvary, the mob had stopped its speed. The soldiers seemed alarmed. Their spears were held at rest. And they were calling loud with oaths for help. My precious Love had fallen once again beneath the cross. I could not see His form nor face. I did not dare to look at Mary then, she trembled so. I pressed her icy hand and tried to speak in signs my truest sympathy. My own poor heart had broken long ago, but what was grief like mine to hers? I tried to part the Mother's mantle folds, that I might see. Oh! will my Blessed One arise again? If He hath fainted now, how can the height of Golgotha be reached? The shadow of the awful hill is here. This cannot be His dying bed!

And then I prayed for grace. My Mother's life seemed passing into mine. Her all-availing lips were moving with my words. The crowd was pressing up the hill. The spears were mounting the ascent. And there before me stood another with my Master's cross. He was wrestling with the heavy load, and, though the blood was rushing to his face, his features seemed suffused with joy. How strange it was to see that cross upon another laid, that blessed wood already moistened with the saving blood! O happy lot to bear the burden for my Love, to stand an instant in His place! And I was weak enough to wish that I had been this chosen soul, that I had been so blest to soothe my Master's weary way, and feel upon my shoulders, too, a portion of His cross. It was my foolish love that counted not the cost, nor knew how little is my strength to suffer or to die.

And now before me stands the hill of Calvary. The soldiers lead the way. The happy Simon struggles with his load. His strength is failing as he mounts the steep ascent, and yet the burden grows more dear at every step. My Blessed Master walks with pain, as if His limbs were dislocated by the fall. I tried in vain to see His face. His head was bowed upon His breast. His breathing came with sighs. The road was rough, the stones were sharp. His feet were bare and bleeding, as if bruised with many wounds. His hands were bound. We passed the gate of judgment then. The soldiers' spears were forcing back the crowd. Beyond the line of staves and swords I saw a little company of friends. The matrons of Judea and maidens fair had come to weep with plaintive tears. They saw the hands in fetters vile that blessed their homes, that healed their sick. The face that smiled upon their sorrowing hearts was pale with agonizing pain. The thorny crown had pierced the bone, and blood with water ran from every point, while tears were coursing down, and mire and spittle filled the swollen mouth. He turned His head. His lips were trembling so that He could hardly speak. They moved convulsively in prayer I thought I heard Him call His Mother's name in faintest tones. He surely tried to see her face. I thought He asked that she might touch Him then, that her dear hands might rest upon His aching brow or wipe away the clotted blood, the spittle and the mire. The hour of death was near. Might not the Mother once again prepare her Child for sleep? Before the nails were driven, before the awful wounds were made, might not her touch compose the limbs and features of her only Son? Oh! how she trembled then! Her hand was colder than the grave. I did not dare to look upon her tearful face. I know not how she quickened then her faltering steps, as we rushed on unmindful of the angry crowd, unmindful of the oaths that gave response to every sigh or tear. So we had nearly reached the summit of the mount where skulls were strewn around, where bones in nauseous decay polluted all the air. It seemed the opening of a charnel-house with all the sickening odor of corrupting flesh. This was the dying bed of Mary's Child, the Word of God!

The Blessed Mother seemed so faint that even I was overwhelmed with fear that she would die! She fell upon her knees and lifted up her eyes to heaven. It seemed the bonds of flesh were breaking then; that she had knelt among the skulls to yield her agonizing soul to God. I never heard such sighs; I never saw such tears. "O Mother dear!" I cried, "oh! leave me not! The love of innocence is here. The love of penitence is at thy side. The end is close at hand. I cannot here abide without thy strength. I cannot see Him die alone. Thou art kneeling now, as pale as death. I would that I could comfort thee in this thy martyrdom. But I am very weak. I can only give thee love, the heart that breaks with thine. Oh! let me help thee up and we will see our Jesus yet; and once again thine eyes shall feast on His. Perhaps the cruel mob will give thee place, will grant a mother's right, and thou shalt touch His hands and feet, and with thy lips shalt kiss Him ere He dies. O thou dearest, holiest of the race of man, thou virgins' Queen, the Mistress of the skies! who can dispute thy sway? The spears must fall at thy command, and thou shalt rule on Golgotha. Oh! let us come; I know the Master calls. I feel the beating of His heart in thine. Courage, Mother dear! for we shall see Him soon."

She looked at me with terror in her face, and spoke with faint and trembling words: "You cannot see, my child. Our Blessed Love has fallen once again, and when I knelt he fell. Listen to the whips wherewith they beat Him now. Oh! hear the curses that resound! They call Him fallen King. They bid Him rise and wear His crown. And I must kneel and pray. I cannot rise until they lift Him up. See, here the holy woman comes to me. She beareth here the awful picture of my Child. The Mother could not touch the sorrowing face, but she receiveth now the offering of His love. And He who is so dear to me hath sent by her this image of my dying Son. Oh! let us look upon that face, so bruised and torn. See here the gashes of the thorns, the marks of clotted blood, the courses of the tears. Behold the anguish of that brow, the lacerated cheeks, the swollen mouth. O my Blessed Child! I take Thy gift, and I will teach Thy spouses dear to keep the watches of their love, to dwell with me upon the treasure of Thy wounds. O precious face! I know it well! I know its every line. Full well I read the features of my darling Son. Oh! who but God can see the pain, the anguish written there? Come kneel with me and here adore the precious blood. Before this agonizing face let innocence its incense bring, let sinners' tears but freely flow. The beauty uncreated and the light of heaven are hidden here. The smile of pardon is the pang of pain; the gifts of grace are bruises here. Oh! let us read that face a moment now before we kneel around the cross, before we strain our fainting eyes to catch its dying glance. I have not here a mother's right. I cannot touch my darling Child until He dies, until they lay the cold and mangled body in my arms, and Bethlehem's ministries return beneath the shadow of the cross. Yet there I shall be once myself again, shall take my Love unto my breast, shall all the ghastly wounds adore, shall kiss the dearest lips with all the ardor of a mother's heart. And even now I seem to feel that touch, and even now before me lies the garden of His grave. See here, my child, He rises from His fall. The cross again is on His shoulders laid. He mounts the summit of the hill. The weary road is ended now. Hear you not the fearful sound that cometh from the caverns of the deep? Feel you not the quaking of the earth as if with living horror moved? And see you not the angry clouds that are the curtains of the sky? See, nature mourns the dying of its Prince. See the awful pall that covers all created things.

"Oh! let us come. The hour is nigh. Some power unseen is bearing me beyond my strength. I see no angels here, and yet I feel their might. They hold me up. They stretch their wings beneath my feet. The wound within my heart is open now and bleeding fast. The Mother's blood is calling to the Son's. Oh! let us hasten for the end. Faint not, my trembling child; these awful hours will try your faith and love. Beneath my mantle hide; hold fast my hand and follow me."

I lifted up my eyes, so red with tears, to see if I could catch my Mother's glance as thus she bade me come. The strangest beauty crowned her brow, and yet it was unlike the glory of the past. It seemed the beauty of a soul that sinks to death in majesty divine. It was a dying face, and yet the image of celestial life. My hand was cold as hers, and as I clasped her fingers dear I felt the earthly life was leaving me; and yet a newer, better vigor came with every breath. I remember naught but this, as together we came near the summit of the hill, and found our way among the stones and skulls of Golgotha. I was lifting up my heart to heaven. I was looking for my Love. The precious name was on my lips. I begged that I might see Him yet before His death, to tell Him of my truth, that I had kept my word, that I was watching to the last. He seemed so near me then, although I saw Him not. O Mother dear! I cried, how gladly would I die, if I might hold thy precious hand; if He, my All, might be so near! The sweetness of His heart is killing me. I hear the voice that openeth heaven. He calleth me with tenderest names. He saith to me: "My sister and My love, My dove, My undefiled, open all thine heart. My head is full of dew, is aching for thy breast. The drops of blood have crimsoned all My hair. See how I lie upon the cross, outstretched upon the ground. I bear the blessed wood no more. The tree of life, it beareth Me. My way of sorrows past, the altar takes the sacrifice. Oh! listen now. They bring Me vinegar and gall. I see the nails; with My own will stretch out My hands and place My feet. The Lamb of God is ready now."

I turned to speak. "Dearest Mother of my Lord, oh! hast thou heard these sweetest words? He never spoke to me like this before. He draws me so that I can hardly live. Oh! I must go and fall beside Him as He lies, and I must tell Him of my love and kiss His feet again. Oh! who can hold me here? Oh! who can tear me from His side? Oh! let me go and die with Him. I do not love thee less—indeed, I love thee more; but He is All to me."

"My child," I heard her say, "I bless thee for thy heart, which here awakes in life that cometh from the cross. How gladly would I go and die with Him, and lead thee to the altar now! The death within His bleeding arms is paradise indeed. When He is gone how shall the Mother live, and what is earth to her who weeps a Child divine? And yet I have no will but His. I take my chalice, too. My heart is pierced with His. My hands and feet are nailed. I lie beside Him on the cruel wood.

"See the ruffians crowd around. See the bristling spears. The fearful work is going on. No friend can pass. Oh! listen to the awful sound. Above the jeer, above the laugh, the hammers strike upon my breast. My fainting nerves are yielding to the spikes that pierce them through. O Jesus mine! how can Thy Mother bear this pang? I hear Thy sighs; I feel the tremor of Thy frame. The faintness that oppresseth Thee is killing me. Oh! let me fall upon my face while Thou art lying there. The Mother's sobs ascend with Thine. The Mother's heart is crucified at last."

Prostrate on the ground I saw my glorious Queen. Her groans awoke me from my foolish, selfish dream. "What can I do for thee, my Mother dear? I did not mean to leave thee in thy woe. I only asked that thou wouldst guide me to my Jesus' feet." And then there came a sickness at my heart, and I had fallen too. Of all that passed the memory is gone save only this. My soul was filled with prayer that gathered all my powers in one. I saw my Master lying on His cross among the skulls. I watched His bed of death. I marked the wounds that held Him fast. I saw the dislocated limbs, and tried to fix upon my heart the features of His precious face. I counted all the thorns that pierced His brow, the bruises on His cheeks. I treasured up the tremors of His mouth, and even looked within His blessed eyes. It was my foolish prayer, and yet I thought as He lay there, and tears were falling fast, He looked at me and smiled. And oh! that smile will never fade from memory's page. Shall I see it once again? Jesus, Master of my soul, Beloved of my heart, oh! shall I see it when I die?

When I came back to consciousness the scene was changed. It was as dark as night on Calvary. Around me torches gleamed. The soldiers' spears were standing full at rest. An awful stillness reigned. The crowd had passed away. Our vigil had begun, and we were watchers at our Jesus' feet. The mournful Mother stood beneath the cross as priestess at the sacrifice. One hand she held upon her breaking heart; the other pointed to her Child. The blessed John was weeping at her side, and Magdalen had fallen prostrate on the ground. The cross was trembling with His dying pangs, and He was lifted up on high and hanging by His wounds.

And I was kneeling at my Mother's side, and we were there alone. She held my hand in hers; she called me child. I hid my grief within her mantle's folds, and heard her tearful, fainting voice: "This is the end. Our weary road leads here. All sorrows drear find here their resting-place, and every light that shines is guiding to the Cross. For this the voice of Gabriel speaks. For this the angels sang on Bethlehem's heights. For this the three-and-thirty years of blessed union with the Word made flesh. For this the joys of motherhood divine. For this I laid Him on my heart and nursed Him at my breast. For this were every fond caress, and every kiss, and every smile. This is the centre of the earth redeemed. Behold Him lifted up. See how He draweth all things to Himself. This is the heavenly Bridegroom's throne. Here souls espoused to Him come home, here celebrate the nuptial rite. Within these shades I reign. I rule where earth departs, and in the midnight of the soul I come as Queen. I lead thee to my Child when thou hast learned to crucify thyself with Him. His parting breath shall bind thee to His side, and thus on Calvary the bridal train shall come. Oh! see how dark it is. The sun hath ceased to shine. The stars are hidden in the blackened sky. The earth is trembling in its fear, and Nature sends from every side her funeral song. The King, the eternal Son, will meet the iron sceptre of the grave, and He will die.

"Draw nearer to the cross. I lead you there. See how the blood is running down. See how each struggling breath is pain. Look up with all your love, with all your faith. Adore the Bridegroom of your heart. Pay Him your vows, and then the watches of your vigil keep. The darkness shall increase until the noon of an unearthly night; but wait in prayer, abide with me, and you shall see the twilight of the dawn."

I lifted up my weary eyes. At first

I could not see. There was an awful silence in my soul. I heard the sobs of Magdalen, the sighs of John, the painful breathing of my precious Queen, as there in all her deathlike majesty she stood. I heard the groans that came so faintly from the trembling cross. Oh! how my Love was suffering then! Oh! that my eyes might see Him once again, and say farewell, when lips could form no words, and every sense was dumb. Jesus, Master mine, Thou heavenly Spouse, oh! give me grace to see. I care not for the clouds. The light of day would mock my grief. But in this night touch Thou my sight, and let me look again upon my only Love. For here my Mother leads me with her gentle hand, and here I plight to Thee my everlasting truth.

I know not how His mercy heard my prayer. The darkness deepened until it seemed that light was dead; and then upon the background of a superhuman night I saw the royal cross, the pale and agonizing form of my Beloved. At first I saw the bleeding feet. The cruel spike had pierced them well. The awful wound was red and swollen round the nail. Convulsions from the fearful pain were tearing wide the ragged gash. I kissed them with my heart. I could not touch them with my mouth. The limbs were thin and pale, and stained with blood, and all the bones seemed dislocated, so that every tremor was a pang. I saw the precious hands that wiped away my tears, the arms divine that often held me in a fond embrace. Oh! they were strained and bleeding, too. The hands were clasping fast the nails, and they were white as death. The breast where mercy finds its royal throne was panting as if life would go. Now there came a breath with anguish keen, and then a moment all was still. The sacred Heart was beating with the speed of light, and then its awful struggles ceased. There came a ghastly paleness, as if death had come. The dear, the precious face was peaceful as the calm of God, and patience reigned where pain had reached its height. My Love was surely dying now. The head is drooping down. The locks are filled with dew and mire and blood. The thorny crown has pierced the brow. The mouth is open wide. The lips are parched and blue. The blessed eyes are sometimes closed, and when the trembling eyelids part the look is far away from earth. Sometimes the lips are moving as to words, and yet I hear no sound.

So as I looked it seemed to me that I was growing nearer to my Lord. I could not rest. I could not still my prayer. "Jesus, Master, Love!" I cried, "accept my vows. This is the bridal hour. Behold Thy spouse for ever Thine and only Thine! Oh! let the nuptial rite proceed."

I looked with all my love upon His bruised and mangled face. I held my hands upon my heart and wept. I thought the precious eyes were opened once. I thought they smiled. I saw new tears run down. I thought He bowed His head to me, and looked as if He heard my vow and made me there His own.

And then the awful cloud returned. The blackness came again. So kneeling at His feet I fell, and all my sight was gone.

The shadows deepened on my heart till sadness worse than death was quenching all the springs of life. My foolish love had hoped to see His dying face, had even prayed to be with Him unto the last. But now I cannot live; I cannot raise my head. I do not dare to look again. How can I see the dearest Master of my soul in such an awful death? I cannot go away; and yet I cannot bear the torture of this awful scene. He is my God! He is my All. He is my only Love. How can I see Him die?

Oh! who will hold me up, that soul and body do not part, that grief like mine consume me not before His parting breath? If I could live until. He dies, and then with Him depart from earth, my only prayer would rise like incense to the blood-stained feet. But oh! I know He is not dying now, and yet my little strength is going fast; my breath is failing me; my breaking heart has ceased to beat. O Mother of my Love! come near. Oh! let me touch thee once again. If I may feel thy precious hand once more, my wasting life may yet return, and I may yet with thee this vigil keep. Oh! help me, Mother blest, and I will be thy child by ties of blood. Together shall our hearts be bleeding here; together shall we watch on Calvary.

I did not know how near to me my glorious Queen was weeping then. I felt the peace her gentle presence brings. I felt the pressure of her loving hand. My soul was calmed. My grief was more intense, and yet I seemed to rest, while peace, the peace of God, was reigning in my pangs. My feverish pulses paused; the anxious panting of my breath had ceased, and in its agony my heart was lying still. And then I heard her voice in tearful tones: "My child, the school of love is here, the school that teacheth to endure. The night is just begun. Through awful shades, through sweat of blood, through every pain that tries the soul, that crushes nerve and flesh, our heavenly Master leads. There is no pang He beareth not, no grief He tasteth not. He dieth as a king; He dieth as a God. The crown of thorns He weareth to the end, and bows His royal head as Prince of life and death.

"Deeper, darker will the shadows grow. The midnight horror yet shall come. It shall be colder than the grave, and every light but His shall die. The child that seeks to keep his vigils here must bid farewell to all created things, must come to lie beneath the funeral pall, must come to seek a burial place among the skulls. Only Jesus here, and Jesus on His cross! For I shall hide myself behind the clouds, and in the unearthly gloom shall only point to Him. Behold my Child, thy Bridegroom and thy King!

"I see how cold thou art. Thy hand is trembling so that I can hardly hold it still. This is indeed the place of death. Here all of earth must die. Oh! wrap thyself within thy shroud and listen to the marriage-bells. So faintly sounding now, they tell thee of thy death in Him thy Life. That death is pain. That death is sweet. The icy grave is portal to the palace of thy Spouse. The wounded hands are waiting for thy last caress. The mangled feet will lead thee to thy home. The bruised and bleeding face will smile when thou art dead to all but Him. The precious lips are yearning for thy loving kiss.

"O cruel death! thou reignest here. O Life of God that in this desert drear, amid the gloom where sun nor stars can shine, shalt rise in worlds of bliss to people heaven with virgin souls, with spouses of the Lamb!"

My dearest Mother ceased her blessed message to my dying heart. I kissed her hand with all the ardor of a newborn life. Some mighty grace was moving in this deep of night. I felt the change that came so strangely then. For surely it was like a death, and yet it was a birth! I did not know myself. I only knew I held my Mother's hand and passed away where, in a world unknown, I saw my Jesus Crucified, and Him alone.

www.ingramcontent.com/pod-product-compliance
Lightning Source LLC
Chambersburg PA
CBHW021204230426
43667CB00006B/546